QUINCY M.E.

── The Television Series ──

JAMES ROSIN

Published in the USA by:
BearManor Media
P O Box 71426
Albany, Georgia 31708
www.bearmanormedia.com

ISBN 1-59393-454-8

Printed in the United States of America.

Book design by Darlene Swanson of Van-garde Imagery, Inc. (www.Van-garde.com)
Cover Design by Ron Dorfman (www.ronalddorfmandesign.com)

ALSO BY JAMES ROSIN

Philly Hoops: The SPHAS and Warriors

Rock, Rhythm & Blues

Philadelphia: City of Music

Route 66: The Television Series

Naked City: The Television Series

Wagon Train: The Television Series

Adventures in Paradise: The Television Series

Contents

FOREWORD

It seems appropriate that Jim Rosin would write about the history of *Quincy M.E.* He was there when shooting began, and through the years contributed stories and teleplays, acted in episodes, and has remained a friend to Jack Klugman even to this day.

Jim has written several other fine works on classic television shows, including *Wagon Train, Route 66, Naked City* and *Adventures in Paradise.* Exhaustive research is one of his strong points. He probes deeply, seeking truth with the intensity of a dedicated medical examiner. If you liked *Quincy M.E.*, you'll love Jim's book. By the time you put it down you will know the basic plot of every episode and meet the key players who kept it on the air for seven seasons. In their own words, you will hear about struggles, conflicts, and the ceaseless pressure they faced each day trying to keep the good ship *Quincy* afloat. Hits are hard to come by. Even harder to maintain.

Near the end of the first season, Jack asked me to write and direct an episode which he hoped would serve as a model for all future episodes. He was desperate for a new focus, one which would not only entertain his viewers but also enlighten them on science, personal responsibility, and the need to root out the moral injustices so pervasive in society. He wanted a message show. The studio wanted a detective show.

Jack spoon-fed me a story idea that preached the importance of proper collection and legal documentation of evidence in rape cases. Many rapists, he insisted, were walking the street because of "breaks in the chain of evidence" that allowed their acquittal. The result of our collaboration was titled "Let Me Light the Way." It aired as the final show of the season, pleased Jack enormously, and gave him new ammunition for his battle with Universal.

Finally, the conflict came to a head at the end of season four; Jack threatened to quit, and the studio said if he did they would sue. Guns were on the table, blood ready to spill. Fortunately, mature reason and South Philly smarts caused Jack to compromise. He told the men in black suits that if they hired me as executive producer, he would continue working. They agreed; I hesitated. As a freelancer for almost twenty-five years, I had written and directed scores of scripts, but never once been a member of any studio staff. I didn't have a clue about what executive producers really did. I was asked to be top gun without ever having strapped on a holster.

Fortunately, "mature reason" — the lure of steady employment — changed my mind. Luckily, the minute I stepped into the *Quincy* offices, I found myself surrounded by talented and genuinely nice people: Bill Cairncross, the veteran post-production supervisor, the man responsible for making a finished product from film shot by our director; Lester Berke, the line producer who knew how to evaluate budgets, hire crew members, and run the logistical end of the show; San Egan, an inspired young writer, child of holocaust survivors, who had single-handedly kept script coming in the previous season (he was able to relate the plots of every show thus far filmed. Thinking back, all I can say is thank God for Sam. Without him, I may have crashed and burned).

Two more key people soon completed our staff. After much
trial and error with freelancers, along came a winner: Michael
Braverman. Not only did he write well, but he had a natural instinct
for the show. Once he found a worthy issue, such as incompetence,
corruption, or misuse of power, he became a bloodhound, sniffing
and sniffing until he got to the bottom of things. Then, no matter
who the wrongdoers were, he pounced. Even the FAA got bitten by
Michael.

Last, but not least, came Jeri Taylor. Sam had worked with her
and introduced me to her at a local delicatessen. I invited her in for
a story pitch, liked her idea, gave her an assignment, and one week
later was delivered a remarkable script. Her writing reflected her
sensitive and compassionate soul. And she was fast! Most writers
take several weeks to hand in a first draft; she did it in seven days.
There was absolutely no way I was going to let her escape. She
wrote some of our best episodes, including a powerful and touching
examination of the emotional journey of a woman dying of brain
cancer.

Within months, Universal's problem child had ceased to kick
and scream. Episodes were being completed on time, on budget, and
best of all, the black-suited executives were no longer getting chilling
phone calls from Jack. Somehow their appreciation never reached
the *Quincy* offices. Old hand Bill Cairncross took me aside and
explained the facts of life. "When you <u>don't</u> hear from them, that's
good. When you <u>do</u> hear from them, that's very bad."

No single person deserves credit for this turnaround. We all
toiled together, struggled together, supported each other and, if
memory serves, drank a little wine at lunch. Because of his relentless
drive for perfection, Jack was not an easy boss. When he disliked
a script, which he often did, you could hear an explosion from his
dressing room across the lot. I distinctly remember a phone call one

Saturday morning at 6:00. Jack had just finished reading a script we were enthusiastic about and needed desperately for production. "I hate it!" he bellowed into my still slumbering brain. "I'm gonna rip it up and throw the blankety-blank pieces in the blankety-blank Pacific Ocean!" I figured he wasn't kidding because at that time he was living on the sands of Malibu Beach.

By the end of our first year together, *Quincy M.E.* was nominated for an Emmy. During the remaining two, we were nominated for a People's Choice Award and honored by numerous organizations that appreciated the messages we were fighting to convey. I remember one such event, a dinner presentation held in the ballroom of a prestigious Beverly Hills hotel. The writers and producers were seated around a large circular table: Jack was happy and relaxed, laughing, joking, enjoying every minute. When the time came for us to go to the podium, I saw him watching with enormous pride and appreciation. We were his children. I remember placing a hand on his shoulder, leaning closer, and telling him that I loved him.

David Moessinger
February 2009

ACKNOWLEDGMENTS

I would like to thank the following people who contributed to this book: Jeanene Ambler, Val Bisoglio, Michael Braverman, William Cairncross, Phil Cook, Bob Del Valle, Ira Diamond, Sam Egan, Don Eitner, Jeff Freilich, Anita Gillette, Jeffrey Hayden, Jack Klugman, David Moessinger, John S. Ragin, Joe Reich, Ron Satlof, Lou Shaw, Jeri Taylor, Mark Scott Taylor, Chris Trumbo, and Harker Wade. Also, very special thanks to Ned Comstock and the USC Cinematic Arts Library.

Author's Note

Many television historians document the *Quincy* television series as having run for eight seasons, counting the first year (1976–1977) as two seasons. I don't, and count the first year as one season. *Quincy* was originally shown as part of the *Sunday Night Mystery Movie* series. After four ninety-minute episodes were telecast (over a period of three months), the series began to air weekly (for an additional four months). For my purposes, the total of sixteen episodes comprised one season. In addition, the show is sometimes listed as consisting of 148 episodes. In actuality, there were 146 produced.

QUINCY M.E.

About the Series

Quincy M.E. debuted on Sunday, October 3, 1976 on the NBC Television Network. Initially, it was telecast as a series of 90-minute episodes in rotation with *Columbo, McCloud,* and *McMillan* as part of the NBC *Sunday Mystery Movie.* After four segments aired, the well-received show began to air weekly on February 4, 1977. *Quincy M.E.* was initially conceived by writer Lou Shaw and developed by both him and producer Glen Larson; Universal studio executive Frank Price later sold the series to the NBC Network. The premise revolved around an investigative medical examiner with a strong sense of principle, who worked for the Los Angeles County Coroner's office.

LOU SHAW
(Creator/Producer 1976 –1977)

> I first conceived the idea several years before
> it became a series. I envisioned Quincy as the
> first medical detective on television. Someone
> who would make discoveries and solve crimes
> forensically. He sought the truth with a dogged
> determination, especially when facts he found
> during the course of his investigation didn't make

sense. His pursuit was relentless, regardless of what the medical examiner's office or police department thought. Quincy felt that part of his job was to see that all the evidence found was utilized, that he owed that to the victim. His business was pathology and he was taught to trust no one. He would take it for granted there was something wrong in every autopsy.[1]

In the premier script, Shaw wanted to write a speech that illustrated the essence of his title character but struggled to come up with it.

LOU SHAW

I remember holding up the script for a day because I couldn't find the right words. Then it came to me in a scene where Quincy wants to exhume a body for examination and a doctor questions why he would specialize in work of this kind when he's qualified to treat the living. Quincy gives him the bottom line: "After all the bull — there's been one thing about life I could never get over — the mystery of it, and something goes tilt in me every time I see life dead before its time. I want to do something about that. I want to find out who made that awful thing happen; and most often, the victim can point the finger in the right direction just as well as if he were still alive; but only if we know how to find it."[1]

Cast in the title role of the determined forensic pathologist was Jack Klugman, fresh from his portrayal of Oscar Madison in *The Odd Couple* TV series. Klugman was an intense and versatile actor adept at both comedy and drama. His roots stemmed from the New York stage, and the role of the persistent medical examiner fit like a glove.

JACK KLUGMAN
(Quincy M.E. 1976 –1983)

>I had a tremendous amount of respect and
>admiration for my doctor, Max Som. I came out of
>an experience with him with the idea that my next
>series could be about a dedicated doctor like him.
>After *Odd Couple* finished in 1975, all the studios
>were telling me that I was a hot property. So I said,
>"Here I am, the next Welby." They looked at me
>like I was crazy. They said, "Don't you know that
>all medical shows are on their way out? How about
>a nice cop show where you're the older cop and
>there's this young cop who's your partner?" I told
>them I didn't want to do another cop show, and I
>didn't want to do another situation comedy. I knew
>that I could never top what Tony (Randall) and
>I had done on *Odd Couple*. They said, "Okay, we
>understand." Then they sent me 65 scripts, every
>one of them a cop show or a sitcom. So I sat out
>most of the 1975-1976 TV season. I did a tour of *All
>My Sons* with Sada Thompson and a TV movie, and
>was content to rest, relax, and spend time with my
>children.[2]

Once *Quincy* was sold to the network and Klugman had agreed to do
the role, NBC ordered the series without making a pilot.

JACK KLUGMAN

>I remember watching a TV interview with Thomas
>Noguchi, the Los Angeles County Coroner who
>was an innovative and brilliant man, one of the
>leaders in forensic medicine. He was talking about

what you could learn from powder burns. All my
life I had heard about them, but never met anyone
who had seen one. Noguchi showed the difference
in a powder burn from a weapon one foot away,
then two feet away, then six feet. It was fascinating.
I had things to do yet I sat glued to the set until the
interview was over.

When I was offered the series, I knew it wasn't
Odets or Arthur Miller, and that Quincy would be
doing detective work, but at least he was a doctor
and I figured I could swing the character more in the
medical direction, solving crimes by forensic and
scientific methods.[3]

A good supporting cast was assembled, and from the outset, a
built-in conflict was established between Quincy and two of the
series regular characters: Dr. Robert Astin (John S. Ragin) his
administrative boss, and Lt. Frank Monahan (Garry Walberg) a
homicide detective for the Los Angeles Police Department.

Initially, Frank Monahan was portrayed as an irascible police
lieutenant under pressure to resolve his caseload, and resentful
of Quincy's determined effort to play detective. Dr. Robert Astin
was a dedicated bureaucrat who walked a fine line between his
administrative responsibilities and keeping his maverick pathologist
Quincy in line.

JOHN S. RAGIN
(Dr. Robert Astin 1976 –1983)

> When the show first began, the producers wanted
> Astin to be on top of Quincy all the time, and at
> one point I began to feel like a heavy. As the show
> progressed, Jack and I began to find the humor in a
> lot of our scenes together, and sometimes we'd re-
> write them accordingly. Humor was a very important
> part of the show because the nature of the series was
> very serious and dramatic. So this gave it balance and
> I believe it broadened the appeal of the show.[4]

Monahan, who resisted Quincy's intrusions, began to welcome his
meticulous detective work and insightful deductions.

Two series characters who allied themselves with Quincy from
the beginning were Sam Fujiyama, his faithful assistant and diligent
lab analyst, and Danny Tovo, owner of Quincy's favorite bar and
meeting place. Robert Ito, who portrayed Sam Fujiyama, was a
quiet, kindly, cheerful and reliable man who provided a much-
needed balance on the set.

JACK KLUGMAN

> Bobby was exactly what the show needed.
> Whenever there was tension, there he was: gracious,
> and someone who never complained or asked for
> more. Instead he was there wondering how he could
> help you. I would have done anything for him.[5]

Ito, a skillful actor with New York stage experience, was content to
play a supporting role in a successful television series. He also took
pride in the warm relationship he established with his co-star, as well
as his understanding of Klugman's temperament.

ROBERT ITO
(Sam Fujiyama 1976 –1983)

> Jack wasn't the type to converse. He would shout.
> Some people would stand up at a table to dominate
> a meeting. Jack didn't take any chances. He'd jump
> up on top of the table.[5]

Val Bisoglio (Danny Tovo) played Quincy's devoted friend and brought a nice change of pace to the series.

VAL BISOGLIO
(Danny Tovo 1976 –1983)

> When the show began, Danny was supposed to be
> the second male banana to Quincy. But Jack wanted
> the show to move in another direction and he was
> right. As a result, my character became less significant.
> At the time I had a theater and other interests in New
> York, and I didn't want to stay in California to work
> one day here and there. So I went to Jack and told him
> the way he envisioned me on the show wasn't going
> to work. But Jack still wanted me to do the series. So
> I came up with an idea. I said, "Let me out when I
> need to go back east or if a worthwhile film comes up
> that I really want to do." His response: "You got it."
> We did a handshake deal and I stayed with *Quincy* for
> the entire seven year run. Because of our agreement,
> I was able to play the father in *Saturday Night Fever*
> and the Indian Chief in *Frisco Kid* to name a few. If I
> happened to be in New York when they needed me,
> I'd fly back to L.A. and work a day or two. In episodes
> where Danny wasn't part of the storyline, Jack and

I would improvise our scenes together. We had a great rapport. We brought humor and freshness to our scenes and they always worked. Danny's bar/restaurant became a nice sidestep from the forensics.[6]

When *Quincy M.E.* became a weekly series, the first two episodes shown were intended to air as part of the *Mystery Movie* series. "Snake Eyes," a two-hour episode, premiered on February 4, 1977. The following week, a 90-minute segment aired, entitled "The Thigh Bone's Connected to the Knee Bone," which won an Edgar Award for writers Lou Shaw and Tony Lawrence.

Ten one-hour episodes followed, airing from February 18 through May 27, to round out the first season. Once the show changed to the one-hour format, Lou Shaw, who had contracted for the initial six shows, left the series. Jack Klugman, who had also signed for six episodes, welcomed the change.

JACK KLUGMAN

When *Quincy* first began airing, our second show was fourth in the Nielsen ratings. But with network preemptions, the series aired sporadically. (Two *Quincy* shows aired a week apart, then none aired for almost two months; then one aired, and no more until over a month later.) I felt *Quincy* should be better as a weekly series rather than an occasional 90-minute episode. If I was going to work that hard on a show, I wanted it to be anchored so people would know when it was on and have the opportunity to watch it.[3]

At that point, creative differences heightened between Jack Klugman and Executive Producer Glen Larson. Larson, who became a highly successful and prolific TV producer in the late 1970s, leaned more toward the entertainment aspect. Klugman wanted more authenticity and a more serious level of drama than Larson had intended for the show he co-created. Larson was also involved with producing other television series as well as developing projects, so a determined Klugman assumed more creative control.

LOU SHAW

> Jack took his work very seriously and wanted to be involved in every phase of the show. He invested a lot of himself and wanted everything to be up to the standards he envisioned for *Quincy*.[1]

JOE REICH
(Casting Director)

> Jack had a lot of artistic integrity. He was an honest man and you always knew where you stood with him. He never hesitated to let you know exactly how he felt. There were times when he was warm and friendly and explosive the next. When people yell and get angry, you respond to their anger and really don't hear what they're saying. But when you got to know Jack, you saw beyond it all; that he was a caring guy striving to do the best he could. I tried to help him in turn by coming up with the best actors I could find for each and every episode.[7]

JACK KLUGMAN

From early on, my big concern was to keep *Quincy* from becoming another cop show. I wanted to do scripts that were relevant and meaningful, that people could watch and learn from. To me that was more entertaining than girls, guns, and car chases.[3]

ANITA GILLETTE
(Dr. Emily Hanover 1982 –1983)

Jack was socially aware. He showed a lot of courage and determination to use his show as a platform to speak on issues that he felt were important and people responded to.[8]

PHIL COOK
(Assistant Director/Production Manager)

A number of our episodes dealt with social issues, but even when the scripts did not have significant social importance, they had relevant storylines with regard to family and situations. I respected Jack for choosing interesting subject matter and using the show to make the public aware of some serious problems.[9]

JACK KLUGMAN

> When we began to do the ten one-hour shows in
> the latter part of the first season, we did one on child
> abuse ("A Good Smack in the Mouth") and another
> on rape ("Let Me Light the Way") that David
> Moessinger wrote and directed.[3]

The story idea for "Let Me Light the Way" came from Marc Scott
Taylor, the series technical advisor. Taylor was involved with a
project to educate emergency room physicians and nurses to collect
the proper evidence in the process of treating rape victims, and how
to deal with their emotional needs as well.

JACK KLUGMAN

> "Let Me Light the Way" was based on a true story
> about a rapist who killed several girls before one
> lived through it and attempted to identify him. But
> the doctors who treated her destroyed any evidence
> of the attack. So the police had to let him go. That
> was quite a story — relevant, true, dramatic and one
> that could bring about legislative change.[3]

During the latter part of that first season, a director that proved
helpful in time of need was Ron Satlof.

RON SATLOF
(Director: Multiple Episodes 1977-1981)

> One of the first scripts I did about social issues was
> "Valleyview," in the spring of 1977. It came just
> before the "rape show," that Jack was very excited
> about doing. However, Jack had concerns about

"Valleyview." He didn't like the story or the way the script was written. All of this came while he was involved in preparing "Let Me Light the Way." So Jack asked me to work with him on "Valleyview" and improvise the script. We rewrote the whole thing, day by day, doing improvisations with the actors. The script supervisor would take down what was said. Eventually when we settled on something, we'd have time to go over subsequent scenes while they were lighting. Christopher Connelly, who played the killer, never knew it until deep into shooting, because we hadn't decided who the killer was.

It gave the show an interesting twist because he genuinely played this sweet, naïve young man until the day we shot the scene where he tried to kill someone. We were able to complete the show on time, and include a good speech by one of the actors on euthanasia which had more meaning than it did in the original script. "Valleyview" turned out very well, and the network reran the show quite often.[10]

Quincy M.E. was filmed in six days (averaging about three days at the studio and three days on location, depending upon the needs of the episode). The permanent sets were housed on Stage 25 at Universal Studios, and consisted of the Medical Examiner's complex (the lab, autopsy room, offices and corridor), Danny's Bar/Restaurant, and Quincy's boat.

Additional sets were built as needed on another stage.

BOB DEL VALLE
(Assistant Director)

> Several factors determined whether a set would be
> constructed for a particular episode (if the studio
> did not already have one standing) or whether a
> practical location would be used. For example, a
> senate hearing room would have to be built because
> nothing like that existed in Los Angeles. In addition,
> a senator's office which was a straightforward four-
> wall set, you would build because it would give you
> more shooting flexibility. If you had Quincy going
> up to someone's house and into their living room,
> you might do that as a practical (location).

> But if you were in the bedroom of a house and
> it would be a tight shoot with not much room,
> you'd do that on a stage. Naturally, the more you
> could keep things on a stage, the more control you
> had. We weighed each situation according to the
> schedule and budget.[11]

IRA DIAMOND
(Art Director)

> Jack was always concerned about the production
> values of the show in terms of how it looked. We had
> several discussions with regard to the permanent
> sets and about making the medical examiner's office
> contiguous. This allowed for scenes to be more fluid
> and have more movement. For example, walking
> down the hall and into a room instead of cutting.

We designed the sets as a complex and constructed them in such a way that the camera would roll through. The doors were double action, mounted on pins rather than hinges, which allowed grips and special effects men to open and close them with a rolling camera. Between rooms, the windows could be tilted for light reflection which was significant.

Attention was also paid to the color of the sets. Back in the mid-70s when we began filming *Quincy*, the studio was still using the big Mitchell cameras and Technicolor film which had a compatibility with shades of blue. However, the L.A. County Coroner's office had lots of green in addition to white. So we decided to put lots of green on the walls which Jack favored. But we took great care to pick shades of green that would reflect harmoniously with the actors' faces and skin tones.

I also spent weeks down at the County Coroner's office learning what kind of equipment to order for lab work and autopsies. Marc Taylor, our technical advisor, oversaw everything we bought and used in the lab.[12]

MARC SCOTT TAYLOR
(Technical Advisor 1976-1982)
(Co-Producer 1982-1983)

Our set was a modern and authentic forensic laboratory complete with a fully operational scanning electron microscope (which allows examination and elemental analysis of the most

minute particles), a gas chromatograph/mass
spectrometer (that could analyze and detect
the minutest trace of poison in a corpse), plus
an estimated one to two million dollars worth
of sophisticated, state-of-the-art lab equipment
periodically on loan from various manufacturers.[13, 14]

In actuality, the series had two technical advisors.

MARC SCOTT TAYLOR

Dr. Victor Rosen (who was a forensic pathologist
at Brotman Memorial Hospital in nearby Culver
City) handled the pathology and I handled the
forensics. Unlike today on shows like C.S.I., we
couldn't show autopsies and body organs, but we
could show all the lab work and that's how I became
involved. When the prop man on *Quincy* came to
my lab and took a tour, I suggested that the show
have a technical advisor. Once they obtained the lab
equipment from the companies I recommended,
they called me to help set things up. Once I did
that, I worked with both Jack and Bob and gave
them things to do in the lab. After that, Jack wanted
me to come back whenever they shot lab scenes.
Eventually I was hired full-time, later joined the cast
and ultimately became a co-producer.[13]

Once on the show, Taylor became an important asset, and
introduced a few forensic procedures of his own. In one episode, he
was able to identify a killer who left no trace except a fingerprint on
his victim's cheek.

MARC SCOTT TAYLOR

> I had worked on a laser technique devised by
> a Canadian scientist that caused fingerprints
> on human skin to emit a fluorescent glow. I
> combined that approach with one perfected by
> Berkeley scientists using some very expensive
> laser equipment on loan. The end result was that it
> enabled Quincy to identify the killer.[14]

In "A Matter of Principle," Taylor devised a procedure that was ultimately used at the L.A. County Coroner's office. In the episode, Sam Fujiyama tries to prove the innocence of a man accused of being a killer-rapist who leaves bite marks on his victims.

MARC SCOTT TAYLOR

> The innocent man is finally acquitted after an actual
> procedure that I devised. It proved with microscopic
> precision that the suspect didn't inflict the puncture
> marks. The photograph of a victim's arm wound that
> appears in the show was one taken of my own arm
> which I bit for the sake of authenticity. You might
> say I really sank my teeth into that case.[13, 14]

In the premiere episode of season three ("The Last Six Hours"), Sam Fujiyama is poisoned, lies near death, and someone is needed to help Quincy determine what type of poison it is.

MARC SCOTT TAYLOR

> Instead of having me teach an actor how to operate
> the equipment which was intricate and expensive,
> they decided that I would play the part of a lab
> technician and do it myself. Jack also felt it was more

authentic to have an actual forensic scientist involved
in the procedures rather than an actor. I remember
my first line of dialog: "Wait a second, Quincy. This
material shows an ultraviolet absorption rate of 280
nanometers. Could it possibly be proteinaceous?"
When I wrote the line I had no idea how hard it
would be to say on camera. My voice must have gone
up two octaves. It was tough, but I got through it,
and it became much more enjoyable as I did more.[13,
14]

In addition to the interior of Quincy's boat (which existed on Stage
25 at Universal), a real boat was used, located in the Marina Del
Rey section of Los Angeles. It appeared in the opening credits and
was used occasionally throughout the first season and beginning of
season two.

HARKER WADE
(Unit Manager 1976 –1977)

The boat was owned by a couple of young lawyers
in Ventura (north of Los Angeles). Originally, we
contracted to use the boat for the first six shows,
then they took it back up north. Once the series
went weekly, the boat had to come back to L.A.
The first idea was to motor it down, but the studio
wouldn't insure it. So we made arrangements to
have it towed down and held our breath. When
the boat arrived, there was only one place which
we finally found that could hoist a boat with that
heavy a tonnage and place it in dry dock in the same
location as before. However, when I went there, the

man who had leased the space to us had disappeared
and the man that took his place knew nothing
about us. Fortunately, I had the paperwork in my
possession because the boat was on its way over. The
man honored it and the boat was placed in the same
exact spot as before.[15]

When *Quincy M.E.* was renewed for a second season (1977-1978),
Glen Larson made his exit and moved on to his other television
series and pilots he was developing at Universal. However, Jack
Klugman continued to do battle with a succession of executive
producers, producers and writers who came aboard.

Fortunately, Klugman had David Shaw as his executive script
consultant, and Irv Pearlberg as his story editor. Both men were able
to work with the series star and rewrite a lot of the scripts that came
in, infusing forensic elements amidst the mystery, drama and humor.
Although many of the 20 shows filmed that season entertained the
viewing audience and garnered good ratings, Klugman longed to do
more relevant and meaningful stories.

At the same time, *Quincy M.E.* never lacked for guest stars.
The series attracted a lengthy list of quality performers such as Van
Johnson, Jane Wyatt, Jose Ferrer, Ann Blyth, Don Ameche, Kim
Stanley, Robert Alda, Carolyn Jones, Lloyd Nolan, Lew Ayres, Barry
Sullivan, Signe Hasso, John McIntire, Jeanette Nolan, Keenan Wynn,
Nehemiah Persoff, Dina Merrill, James Gregory, Craig Stevens,
Lola Albright, Jack Kelly, Robert Webber, Martin Balsam, Anne
Francis, Cameron Mitchell, Julie Adams, Dane Clark, Ina Balin, Carl
Betz, June Lockhart, Stuart Whitman, William Prince, John Saxon,
Brock Peters, Robert Loggia, Monte Markham, James Wainwright,
Jack Ging, Edd Byrnes, Carol Lynley, Carol Rossen, Henry Darrow,
Peter Brown, Jessica Walter, Philip Abbott, John Dehner, Edward

Andrews, Joseph Campanella, Robert F. Simon, Skip Homeier, Moses Gunn, Rosemary DeCamp, Keene Curtis, Joe Maross, Charles Aidman, Keye Luke, Phillip Pine, Elisha Cook Jr., Marshall Thompson, David Opatoshu, Clu Gulager, Peter Mark Richman, John Vernon, Gerald S. O'Loughlin, John Larch, Whit Bissell, Tom Troupe, Carol Cook, H.M. Wynant, Anthony Eisley, Harry Landers and Nick Georgiade. The show also featured a group of up and coming performers such as Donna Mills, Robert Foxworth, Tyne Daly, Barry Newman, Joan Van Ark, Sam Groom, Jo Ann Pflug, Ed Begley, Jr., Melinda Fee and Katherine Justice.

The popularity of *Quincy M.E.* was far and wide, including places you wouldn't expect.

WILLIAM CAIRNCROSS

I was vacationing in Scotland with my wife during our hiatus in 1980 when I accidentally took my eyes off the road and plowed into this van full of Belgian Gypsies. A woman passenger got out and was very angry and verbally abusive. A nearby resident saw the commotion and called the police. When they arrived, the woman went off on them as well. Then my wife got out of our vehicle, and she happened to be wearing her *Quincy* jacket. When the lead policeman saw the jacket and found out I was a producer on the show, he ignored the situation at hand and began asking all these questions about the series and Jack Klugman. At one point, the policeman looked at me and said, "How fast was the van going when it backed into you?" Quincy reached across the Atlantic and saved me from going to jail.[16]

JOE REICH

I remember walking through Macy's in New York and I happened to be wearing my *Quincy* belt buckle that Jack had given me one Christmas. All of a sudden this salesman stopped me and said in earnest, "You should be very proud to wear that belt buckle." I already was. *Quincy* was one of the best shows I cast in my thirty-year career.[7]

JEFFREY HAYDEN
(Director: Multiple Episodes 1979 –1981)

I directed a show about a potential outbreak of botulism at a sports stadium. Quincy traces the source to the underground pipes that contaminated the water supply. So people drinking from the water fountains were getting sick. To this day, nearly 30 years after the show aired, my wife will never drink from a water fountain, and every time she sees me go to one, she does her best to prevent me from drinking from it.[17]

The show's notoriety could also have a reverse effect — as it did on actor Charles Aidman.

JEFFREY HAYDEN

Jack had a very well-written episode about incest ("Nowhere to Run") that he wanted me to direct. The network had refused to do it, but Jack was determined and won out. After I read it, I told Jack I knew an actor who was the perfect choice for the father: Charles

Aidman. Jack knew Chuck, agreed that would be a great piece of casting, so we sent him a script. Chuck was reluctant to do the role. He was doing voice-over commercials for American Airlines, and his contract had some kind of morals clause he was concerned about. I honestly didn't see a problem. He was playing a part. I said, "Chuck, it's a terrific role and I don't think there's ever been a show done like this on TV in terms of the whole problem. Jack fought the networks to get it through. I think you'll make a heck of a statement for yourself as an actor."

Well, he did the show, he was excellent in the part; the episode was outstanding and received a great deal of attention. As a result, Chuck lost his contract with American Airlines. I felt so bad that I had persuaded him to do it and that it worked out the way it did. Fortunately, Chuck was a fine talent and I was able to cast him in other shows that I directed.[17]

During the course of season three (1978-1979) the series featured a number of shows that dealt with social issues and relevant topics such as autism ("A Test for Living"), affirmative action ("Death by Good Intentions"), venereal disease ("A Small Circle of Friends"), the illegal sales of prescription drugs ("Walk Softly Through the Night"), negligent cosmetic surgery ("The Depth of Beauty"), environmental pollution ("An Ounce of Prevention") and alcoholism in the medical profession ("Physician Heal Thyself").

Peter J. Thompson became the new executive producer and brought some stability by recruiting executive script consultant Robert Crais, a superb writer, and story editors Aubrey Solomon and Steve Greenberg who were diligent and productive.

Once a script was ready to be filmed, the director chosen became a significant figure. He would be creatively involved in telling the story, and responsible for the arrangement and composition of all the visual images his audiences would see.

Klugman found comfort and compatibility with directors Ray Danton, Georg Fenady, Ron Satlof and others such as Jeffrey Hayden, Paul Krasny and Corey Allen. There were reasons why.

RON SATLOF

> There were some directors that were capable craftsmen, but they really didn't do that extra bit of homework, and as a result didn't have a proper understanding of the show. They might go to shoot a scene and if Jack asked them a question, they might not have the answer because they really didn't know what the scene was about. At that point, Jack lost patience. I always came very well prepared knowing the material, and at the same time I was open to Jack's ideas. If Jack had a strong opinion about something, he wasn't shy about telling you. Yet he was a very good listener (there were some series stars who were not), and he appreciated a valid point of view. There was always good discussion, and frequently he would make an accommodation for something I wanted. I'm not sure of the exact proportion of who got their way more, but it always felt very fair to me.[10]

Preparation and knowledge of the material proved essential when Ron Satlof was casting "A Test for Living," the first episode filmed for the third season which concerned an autistic child.

RON SATLOF

I auditioned three child actors for the part of Timmy Carson, the 9-year-old autistic boy. I blindfolded each actor, told them I was lighting a match, and instructed them to tell me when they felt warmth near their hand. I assured them they would not get burned and that there was no need for concern. When I lit the match and asked the first two actors if they began to feel anything, they both flinched (even though the match was nowhere near them). The third actor did not. What I found was a child actor who would respond to actual stimuli and not anticipate what shouldn't be anticipated. It provided a good indication of his sensibility and showed where he could stay concentrated and only respond to what he was supposed to respond to. His name was David Hollander, he played the autistic child and he was terrific in the role.[10]

Quincy continued to feature controversial storylines during its fourth season (1979-1980). The premiere episode, "No Way to Treat a Flower," made a powerful statement and led the Environmental Protection Agency to take colchicine, a potentially lethal marijuana-related chemical, off the market.

JEFF FREILICH
(Executive Story Consultant 1979)

Before I began writing for television, I had gone to medical school and learned a considerable amount about forensic medicine. Both Chris Trumbo (my writing partner at the time) and I felt we could come up with some story ideas for *Quincy*. So I arranged a meeting with the newly-appointed executive producer whom I had known from the *Baretta* series.

Before our meeting I had seen an ad in an issue of *High Time* (a popular drug culture magazine in the late 1970s) for colchicine in its free form to be used as a fertilizer for marijuana plants. In reality, colchicine was a chemical that could multiply the chromosomal content of a plant to make it stronger and more powerful. It was also lethal and could kill a person in dosages of 15 milligrams and up.[18]

CHRISTOPHER TRUMBO
(Writer)

Our concern was that there were a lot of people out there trying to increase the potency of their marijuana with this deadly substance.[19]

JEFF FREILICH

What made it interesting and appropriate for *Quincy* was that it was virtually untraceable unless you tested for it specifically, which was remote and far-fetched. Our "colchicine idea" was well received. So now we had a premise about poison marijuana but we needed to build a story. What Chris and I decided was to do everything we felt Quincy would do to get rid of this drug. So I called the FDA (Food and Drug Administration), the DEA (Drug Enforcement Agency), FBI, local police and everyone else involved with the trafficking of drugs. Everyone gave us the same answer: "It's not my department." Finally a lady at the Environmental Protection Agency showed concern. She said she could re-classify colchicine in the form being advertised as a pesticide because it was being used directly on plants. Under that classification, the EPA would have jurisdiction over the sale and they would pursue the people who placed the ad in the magazine. The EPA was able to eventually track them down and the ad along with the people selling it disappeared.[18]

CHRISTOPHER TRUMBO

The story we wrote had Quincy striving to save the lives of the young people involved as well as the young man who had grown the colchicine that inadvertently killed his friends. Quincy also set out to get this substance off the market and in the process goes through the same situation we did.[19]

Freilich and Trumbo worked briefly as script consultants on the show, and then left when other opportunities arose. Freilich was offered a position as a writer/producer on The Incredible Hulk, and at that point his association with *Quincy* was over — or so he thought.

JEFFREY FREILICH

By the time "No Way to Treat a Flower" began filming, a new executive producer had replaced the one that hired Chris and me. He decided to change the ending of our script. The original finale had the young man who was selling the colchicine burning all of it in the woods over guilt of what he had done. Quincy pulls him away from the lethal smoke and saves his life. The new executive producer decided that the young man should roll the world's biggest joint out of newspaper, and when Quincy arrives to rescue him, tell the medical examiner if he takes one step closer, he'll light up. That made our ending bizarre and melodramatic. When I learned of the planned change, I went to see Jack. He agreed with me that the new ending was not in keeping with the credibility of what we had done, which was important to him. Our legitimate ending prevailed. The executive producer did not.[18]

Season four got off to a rocky start. Peter Thompson had left the show at the end of season three to take an administrative position with the studio. Robert Crais, Steven Greenberg and Aubrey Solomon contributed several freelance scripts but were no longer on staff. Their departure left a big void. Executive producers came and went, and for most of the season, the show functioned without one.

WILLIAM CAIRNCROSS

I remember one E.P. (executive producer) had come from a supervising background but didn't have good story sense. Another E.P. was very egocentric and tried to assume too much control. That couldn't work because Jack was already in control. He needed someone to work with him, complement what he did and make the show better. A third E.P.'s ego was in the right place but his writing skills weren't. In addition, freelance writers came to us who really didn't understand our show and were unable to make the kinds of changes and revisions that Jack wanted.[16]

JACK KLUGMAN

I would get up at five o'clock in the morning, come to the studio, shoot the show, rewrite scenes, meet with writers and argue about upcoming scripts that weren't done the way we had agreed they would be, and be the last to leave. Then I'd go home and nothing had been resolved for the following day. All my fighting had been for the moment, for that day, and the next day it would start all over again.

When you worked in the theater and were in a good play, you were on it for months. Out of all the discussions and sometimes arguments, you had time for selectivity, which is the only tool you have as an artist. Then you'd settle into the run, grow and enjoy. In doing a TV series, there was a fight every hour; and when it was over, it was only that one issue you settled, not one that set a precedent for every other day. That was a tough situation to be in week after week, year after year. At one point, I said to myself, "I don't want to do this. Why don't I quit? Why continue to have this floating anxiety? I've gotten everything I wanted, haven't I? Even more than I ever dreamed of? What is it?"

I could never find the answer. I just knew that I had to, as you do in acting, keep it open. Not settle.

Never set your performance; never set your life. It was difficult to explain to someone who would say, "What do you have to complain about?" I'd say, "I'm not complaining. I'm searching; and I hope I never stop."[20]

Ironically, season four would prove to be a pivotal year on *Quincy M.E.* Amidst the myriad of conflicts that arose between Klugman and the studio, important shows would get done, compromises would be few, and an exciting and collaborative time would occur between the series star and a young writer named Sam Egan.

SAM EGAN
(Writer/Producer/Supervising Producer 1979 –1983)

In the fall of 1979, I was approached by two *Quincy* story editors,. to do a freelance script for *Quincy*. I met with the new executive producer and the bones of a story for "Never a Child" were worked out. But the deadline was severe. I had two days to deliver a script. I delivered it on a Friday morning, and by the next morning I received word from the story editors that I would be offered a staff writing job on *Quincy* on Monday based on the producer's delight over the script. When Monday arrived, I learned that Jack had read the script, was very unhappy with it, and essentially killed it, along with any prospect of a staff job. I shrugged it off.

A couple of days later, I heard from an executive at Universal who said that Jack had asked to meet with me about the script. I met with him later that day at Hollywood Park, the racetrack where they were shooting that day. It was a meeting I'll never forget. Jack started ranting about how the story lacked authenticity, and that I should talk to a New York priest who had opened a shelter for teen runaways. I said sure. I knew of the priest and had spoken to him in my quick-start research. Jack's demeanor instantly changed. He told me exactly what he wanted in the episode and I told him I embraced his notes completely.

Two days later I met with Jack in his dressing room/ office and we further refined the script. Meanwhile, I learned that both the executive producer and his staff were out.

Over the next few weeks and months, I wrote script after script for the show, including controversial episodes on incest and elder abuse. I also did a pass on every freelance script that went before the cameras. There was no one at the helm of the show other than Jack himself. We met almost every day and crafted episode after episode. Jack's passion and my fatigue high fueled it all.

At one point I was writing an act a day and delivering the pages to Jack on the set. One day he addressed the whole crew and introduced me as the writer who was keeping the show afloat.

During those months, Jack was embroiled in a contractual dispute with the studio and I was called in by the head of television at Universal, who told me that if I could convince Jack to agree to finish the season, that "there would be something nice in my Christmas stocking." Though Jack settled his differences with the studio, I never got the Christmas bonus.

But my friendship and artistic collaboration with Jack were sealed. My wife and I named our first home "The House that Jack Built."

It wasn't until season five when David Moessinger came aboard that the pressures of keeping the show in scripts fell to shoulders other than just my own.

The collaboration was not without its fireworks. When we did the Edgar Allen Poe award-winning "Stain of Guilt" I learned that "hopping mad" wasn't just an expression. I actually saw Jack jumping up and down on the set when he was making a point to me. Needless to say, it made an impression. But it was never mean-spirited, no matter how lively the debate got. It was always Jack's integrity and passion that drove his insistence on quality.[21]

Overall, *Quincy* became a series that dealt with many controversial issues and, through the power of television, called attention to some very important problems that affected the public and various segments of society.

RON SATLOF

"A Test for Living" had some very important implications at the time we filmed it in June of 1978. There was a growing concern about the difference between people who were mentally challenged and those who were autistic. After the show aired, the studio was flooded with inquiries about autism. One state (and possible more) passed a law regarding the education and treatment of autistic children because a legislator had seen the episode.[10]

After writing episodes that dealt with child pornography ("Never a Child") and incest ("Nowhere to Run"), Sam Egan wrote "Honor Thy Elders," a show about elderly abuse that would bring about unanticipated social change.

SAM EGAN

Jack's brother Maurice had researched and established a number of contacts in the world of the elderly abused. Jack was very passionate about the subject, so he and I basically crafted a story that would have the threads of the social issue that was so important; but also keep it character-driven, a medical mystery, and maintain all the other requirements that would make it a *Quincy*.

Once the show was put together and well received, I began to understand the power of what we were doing. The show was shown on the floor of the Missouri State legislature just prior to a vote on protecting elderly citizens from abuse by other adults. It was some of the first legislation in the country. When the bill passed, State Senator Harriet Woods gave us a lot of the credit for setting the tone and informing the legislators about this important issue. She said our episode presented the need far better than any speech or printed material could have done.

> That was icing on the cake for me, to be working
> in an exciting business and doing important shows
> that actually had some impact on the world. That
> would later be played out in even more grand fashion
> when we did the two shows on Tourette Syndrome
> ("Seldom Silent, Never Heard") and orphan drugs
> ("Give Me Your Week").[21]

After four seasons and 82 episodes, Klugman was weary from the
constant battles with the studio and continuous responsibilities he
shouldered. There was no sign of the ideal executive producer within
sight until one day Marc Taylor approached the series star with a
possible candidate.

MARC SCOTT TAYLOR

> I told Jack that he really needed an executive
> producer with a good story mind — in essence, a
> writer, and someone who shared his vision. He had
> never had that, and I felt it would make a difference.
>
> My choice was David Moessinger, probably one of
> the best writers we ever had on the show. There were
> many writers who came and went. The difference
> with David was that he could not only write a
> beautiful script; he could also make it work with
> Jack. He was versatile and had the ability to take and
> weave the truth into a dramatic situation. A lot of
> writers who crossed our path could write something
> dramatic but couldn't keep it factual. David had that
> capability. Sam Egan was similar to David in that
> he could take elements that were factual and weave
> them into a brilliant story.[13]

Moessinger became executive producer and began his search for writers. He brought in freelancers, gave them assignments and, through trial and error, built an exceptional staff composed of Sam Egan, Michael Braverman and Jeri Taylor who understood the show and shared Moessinger's vision.

MICHAEL BRAVERMAN
(Story Editor 1980–1981; Writer/Producer 1981–1983)

> A lot of freelancers would come in and try to sell us a crime and forensics show. That's not what *Quincy* was about. It was a show about humanity disguised as a crime and forensics show. The important element was what *Quincy* wanted to bring to the public's attention. That's what I would concentrate on. Whether it was the way we treat the people who were children of a lesser God (like young people with Down Syndrome) or people being tossed into the sea without life rafts, or simply the downtrodden. Jack was a humanist and sharing that was the key. The crime and forensics were sometimes the last things I would bring into the script.[23]

Quincy went from a troubled show to one of the smoothest running on the Universal lot. However, even with a good writing staff and harmonious working relationship with series star Klugman, a huge challenge still existed for David Moessinger.

DAVID MOESSINGER

> One of the biggest obstacles was to come up with a concept for a show which had been on the air for many years. Once you had one and liked the idea, you'd write

a ten-page story treatment and present it to the studio
for their approval. Next came network approval. In
the process you'd get notes from both the studio and
network that could be contradictory. Then you'd have
to work out a solution, develop a first draft, present it to
Jack, get his notes, rewrite and revise. Once done, you
might face problems from the production side. Could
we shoot the script in the time allowed? Did it fit the
budget? It would literally take months to go from a
story idea to complete a finished script.[22]

In preparing scripts and developing stories, Moessinger found out
his background as a writer/director served him well as an executive
producer.

DAVID MOESSINGER

I knew from directing that there were a myriad of
problems in night shooting. It took four to five times
longer to light and shoot a scene at night than it did
in the daytime. If there were only two work lights
on, people wandered away and it became hard to
find them. Unless it was a pivotal point in the plot
where you had to have the scene, I found a way to
do it indoors or during daylight. This facilitated
production and one of the reasons why our shows
came in on time, on budget, and Universal liked that.
I never became an executive producer that existed for
my own artistic triumph. I waned to do as good a job
as anyone; yet, I felt a responsibility to the studio to
bring my shows in on time and on budget. They were
paying a huge amount of money to do these shows.[22]

During the final three seasons, several significant episodes were written by Sam Egan, who penned 22 *Quincy* installments overall. "Bitter Pill" was an award-winning episode about look-alike drugs which led to California joining a growing number of states prohibiting their sale. "Seldom Silent, Never Heard" and its sequel, "Give Me Your Week," led to series star Klugman appearing before the U.S. House of Representatives' subcommittee on Health and Environment in Washington, D.C. There, he testified about the so-called "orphan drugs" issue. "Orphan drugs" are those that would provide cures for certain serious diseases, however the pharmaceutical manufacturers felt there were not enough people who suffered from these diseases to warrant the expenditure of large sums of money to develop, perfect, and market them. Congressman Henry Waxman, Chairman of the sub-committee, invited Klugman to appear after learning that Egan's episode ("Seldom Silent, Never Heard") dealt with one of those diseases, Tourette Syndrome, a neurological disorder that affects approximately 100,000 Americans.

SAM EGAN

> The inspiration for that show came from Jack. He alerted me to some research that was done and shared with me what he knew on the subject. Subsequently, I met a young man from a show business family who suffered from Tourette Syndrome. He was a very genial, intelligent young man named Adam Seligman. A lot of the initial groundwork I did for the show was through conversations I had with Adam telling me how he was affected, observing how he was affected, the medications he received, and the overriding issue of "orphan drugs."

> For me, the show was particularly memorable in
> that I did a first draft based on conversations with
> Jack about the story; and when I handed in the
> script, he called me down to his trailer to say that I
> basically hit it out of the park; that it had everything
> he wanted. That was a gratifying moment for me,
> the fact that Jack was so on-board with what I did. It
> energized me for all of the work I did for the rest of
> the season.[21]

An important factor in the eventual success of "Seldom Silent, Never Heard," lay in the casting of the pivotal role of Tony Ciotti, a young man afflicted with Tourette Syndrome. This time Jack Klugman's penchant for authenticity presented a problem for director Jeffrey Hayden and casting director Joe Reich.

JEFFREY HAYDEN

> Once I read the script, I met with Joe (Reich) and
> we came up with several good names for the role.
> Then I heard that Jack was determined to use the
> college roommate of his nephew (or cousin) that had
> Tourette Syndrome. Jack felt that because the boy
> actually had Tourette he would be great in the part.
> Well, I sat down with Joe and voiced my concerns.
> This character carried the show. It was a tour de
> force role and we really needed an actor for the part.
> I had six days to film the script. I couldn't do it with
> a college kid who had never acted before. Not only
> would he have to know his lines and hit his marks,
> but he'd have to make a huge emotional investment
> as well. There was a confrontational scene where he'd
> fight with his father, break down and cry.[17]

JOE REICH

In my opinion, the problem with casting a person with Tourette Syndrome was that the audience would be very uncomfortable watching someone actually afflicted go through the uncontrolled outbursts, facial tics and the rest. It would be very difficult and they would not want to watch it unless they were caregivers. Watching an actor play the part would enable the viewers to stay with the story and become involved. A good actor would take his audience through the emotions, tears and laughter. They'd forget they were watching an actor because he'd submerge himself into the character. It's verisimilitude. The appearance of truth versus the real truth. I wouldn't buy a ticket to see a drunk on stage in a Eugene O'Neill play, but I'd surely watch someone like Jason Robards do it, because he's portraying it.[7]

JEFFREY HAYDEN

As it happened, we then met a terrific young actor named Paul Clemens. He came in, auditioned and knocked us off our feet. When we went to Jack he was still determined and felt the boy with Tourette Syndrome would be fine. But I persisted and Jack in his infinite wisdom agreed to do a reading with our young actor. It went well. Jack agreed with us, said okay, and Paul was terrific in the show.[17]

The sequel to "Seldom Silent, Never Heard," "Give Me your Week," was filmed a year-and-a-half later and had even greater impact.

SAM EGAN

After we did "Seldom Silent," Jack had conversations with Rep. Henry Waxman and the issue remained very much alive within him. So he came to me with the idea of doing a follow-up, honing in on the politics and issues of the pharmaceutical companies regarding their obligations and what role the federal government would have. We fashioned a story that was very ambitious and by the end of the episode we had laid out a very compelling argument for action on the part of Congress to pass a bill in favor of "orphan drugs" because of all the good it could do.[21]

BOB DEL VALLE

One of the highlights of the episode was a protest rally that was a dynamic sequence. Supposedly it took place in Washington, D.C., but we filmed it in Pasadena.[11]

SAM EGAN

One of the extraordinary things in filming that scene, aside from gathering 500 people afflicted with various ailments to play the protesters, was the building of a platform and set to provide a point of view of the crowd.[21]

BOB DEL VALLE

The art department constructed a Washington D.C. Senate office set on a stage at Universal Studios. After the majority of the scene was filmed on that set, a couple of those set walls, including one with a window, were moved onto a thirty-foot tall platform that had been erected on a street in Pasadena. Those set walls were positioned in such a way as to allow the window wall to look out onto the length of that street, which was doubling for a wide Washington D.C. boulevard. This street was closed off for our filming, which was accomplished on a Saturday.

To complete the part of the scene that couldn't be shot on stage, we filmed Jack Klugman and actor Simon Oakland walking over to the window, looking outside, and seeing (and revealing to our cameras) the protest march of 500 participants (all of whom in real life had a strong vested interest in the passage of the orphan drug bill) coming down the street directly towards them. Another six cameras, including one on a 30-foot camera crane, and several handheld cameras were positioned in various places to cover the action of the passionate marchers.[11]

SAM EGAN

The amount of resources that were committed to filming the scene was because Jack wanted it. The studio thought the nature of the material made them look good, so they signed off on it. It was quite an undertaking and an amazing scene to watch come alive.[21]

All of the gratification came when Congress finally passed an "Orphan Drug Act" shortly after the show aired. It gave pharmaceutical companies tax breaks to take up the search for cures to rare diseases and President Ronald Reagan signed it.

Story Editor Michael Braverman (who later became producer during seasons six and seven) tackled such controversial topics as airplane safety ("Scream to the Skies") and Down Syndrome ("For Love of Joshua").

JACK KLUGMAN

My brother Maurice read about the lack of safety equipment on a lot of airplanes that take off over water. He found a former pilot in Florida who had been crusading for this kind of safety equipment. They got together and decided it was something that should be brought to the public's attention. Then my story editor, Michael Braverman, came up with a good scenario and wrote an ambitious teleplay that turned out to be a very powerful show.[24]

MICHAEL BRAVERMAN

When we talked to the FAA, we were told that according to their tests and statistics, life rafts were not necessary in planes that just flew over water when taking off. But the planes could go as far as 117 miles out into the ocean with just a flotation pillow. That wouldn't keep you up, and in 30 minutes the heat of your body gets used up in the cold water and you'd develop hypothermia.[23]

JACK KLUGMAN

It always amazed me that when many industries and corporations had a choice between profit and public safety, they'd go for the profit. If a company makes $200 million and they're polluting a stream, what's the difference to them if they make $195 million and don't pollute the stream?[24]

MICHAEL BRAVERMAN

"For Love of Joshua" was a very important show for me. Everyone wanted to do it, and I wanted to see what I could do to use the platform of television to change people's perception of Down Syndrome. Show that the people who were afflicted could have a happy, healthy, wonderfully productive life; and that we should allow them to have the pursuit of happiness. We as a society misinterpret what illness is, and we shy away from it. Much of the final year of my subsequent series *Life Goes On* was about AIDS and HIV. To acclimate people to say "Look, this could happen to any family at any time, and you have to give the people afflicted the compassion that they deserve." In the case of Down Syndrome, we're talking about someone with an extra Y chromosome. Otherwise, they're just like us.[23]

Another Braverman script gave dramatic expression to a topic in national debate at the time. The subject: the merits of the "not guilty by reason of insanity" defense in criminal trials. "Into the Murdering Mind" has Quincy involved in a case where a young mental patient murders his family. "The boy is sick," his psychiatrist maintains. "The

Boy is a cold-blooded killer" counters the prosecutor. When the prosecutor is unable to prove that the young man knew what he was doing at the time of the killings, the defendant is sent to a mental facility from which he could be released in a matter of months if the doctors declared him mentally fit to return to society.[25]

Braverman's script argues for the change in law that had been suggested during the attempted assassination of President Reagan, whereby jurors could render a verdict of "guilty but insane." Criminals so judged would begin serving their sentence in a mental institution. If they were later found to be sane, they would finish their term in prison.

MICHAEL BRAVERMAN

"Into the Murdering Mind" was based on a true story of a heinous crime committed by a man upon his release from a California mental institution. The man had been institutionalized on the insanity plea for a similar crime. Shortly after he was judged sane and let out he killed a small child. The victim's grandmother related her story to me, and I was motivated to do a script based on this very disturbing situation.[23]

At the request of Senator Strom Thurmond who introduced legislation to narrow the insanity defense, Jack Klugman presented a copy of the program to members of the Senate Judiciary Committee in Washington, D.C. Klugman shared a growing concern with the public about the rights of victims and law-abiding citizens to be protected from convicted criminals whose mental health or rehabilitation could not be assured.

JACK KLUGMAN

> As the Hinckley trial demonstrated and as the *Quincy* episode noted, different experts can reach different conclusions about the same evidence. So if it is a toss-up (as to the defendant's sanity), why give the killer the benefit of the doubt? Why not give those of us who haven't done anything wrong, the benefit of the doubt for a change?[25]

Two important episodes written by Jeri Taylor included "The Night Killer" concerning Sudden Infant Death Syndrome, and "Gentle into That Good Night," about dealing with death.

JERI TAYLOR
(Writer/Story Editor/Producer 1979 –1983)

> A very dear friend of mine lost her child to Sudden Infant Death Syndrome. I remember it hit me very hard, but I don't recall if that was what made me want to write it or if it was a concept that Jack had. It was a very important topic. With unfortunate frequency parents were being accused of having done something to their child because it was not understood that a child could die for no apparent reason.

> "Gentle into That Good Night" was probably my favorite episode because it was such a personal story. It approached death in a straightforward way that I had never seen on television. It made a point that as a society we try to avoid any thought of it and sanitize it. In the past, people lived much closer to the concept

of death. They laid out the dead in their home. It was a much more personal thing. Today it's fallen into disfavor and we shrink from it. That's why this show was so meaningful.[26]

WILLIAM CAIRNCROSS

"Gentle into That Good Night" was 72 minutes in first cut. We tried to get the network to air it as a 90-minute special because it was an important script. NBC said no, so we had to cut out nearly a third of the footage to fit the hour time slot which was 48:30.[16]

DAVID MOESSINGER

I directed the episode and I vividly remember the finale. It opened on the sun bursting through the trees and panned down to the family at graveside. The final shot came from an upward angle as Quincy and Dr. Pendleton (a specialist on dealing with the dying) came up the hill. Pendleton (Michael Constantine) had a quote that meant so much to me because it typified our life cycle where the patient says, "Doctor, doctor, will I die?" and the doctor replies, "Yes, my son, but so will I." They moved past camera as we looked down the rolling hillside to the dotted gravestones below. It was a beautiful perspective.[22]

WILLIAM CAIRNCROSS

Jack wanted to eliminate the funeral scene. He felt it was a cliché and wanted to go right to the final shot of Quincy and Dr. Pendleton coming up the hill. In review, I found that eliminating an unnecessary scene that preceded the funeral scene gave it a fresh perspective.

Prior to the funeral scene were two scenes. First in the hospital where Kay Silver (Tyne Daly) is dying and wants to go home. Her husband, reluctant for emotional reasons, finally embraces her and says something to the effect of "Let's go home." We cut to a close-up of Kay and a tear rolling down her cheek.

The next scene is at their house where we see the kids playing and Kay cooking. There was the problem: it was extraneous and anti-climactic to go from that beautiful hospital scene where husband and wife come together regarding her approaching death to that scene at home, and then to the funeral.

So from her face in the hospital room, I did a long dissolve to the sun bursting through the trees and panning down to everyone at graveside. The funeral scene now worked, setting up that wonderful hillside shot finale without dissipating any emotion. When I ran the final cut there wasn't a dry eye in the house. Jack stood up and nodded his head with a gentle smile. That was an example of what I learned from him about storytelling and what he learned from me and my crew about what could be done on film with regard to that storytelling.[16]

JACK KLUGMAN

The final three years of the series I had four
wonderful writers on staff, and I had no problems
with the network or studio. But it was still difficult
to come up with the kind of material I wanted to do
week after week. My complaint was the lack of time
these talented people had to write. We had to create
one show every seven days and they were constantly
under pressure. When you have to do 22 scripts,
and you have time constraints, you're in trouble. It
doesn't matter who you can get to be on the show
or how good the writer is. Time can be an enemy to
artistry.[24]

The real pressure of doing a weekly series also presented problems
for the actor. It became difficult for a lead actor to prevent himself
from becoming stale due to constant repetition.

JACK KLUGMAN

The only way you could try to prevent that was to
get scripts that involved you in different ways on
a personal level. One example was a show called
"Touch of Death." Sam didn't want me to perform
an autopsy on a Japanese victim. It violated his
cultural tradition. I told him I had to, he became
resentful, and quit his job. Then I had to resolve
my relationship with him. We had some very tough
scenes and I believe some very good ones.[20]

However, finding ways to stretch as an actor on a long-running series was virtually impossible. That proved frustrating to the group of actors like Klugman that came from the New York theater.

JACK KLUGMAN

The best thing to do was to forget it, but I always had trouble doing that. My early training was like an albatross around my neck. When I began, there was no television. So you had to compete in a business that really offered only a few jobs. You had to know Ibsen, Shaw, and Chekhov. You learned how to start with a character, develop it, and build it. We developed an enormous amount of knowledge about our craft. Then series television said, "We only need a quarter of an inch. We don't need the rest." Nobody cared about your 34 years of experience. They'd say "Do a good job; but do it in six days." So you'd commit to doing everything you could to make it the best it could be, knowing that most of the time a minimum of your talent, technique and experience were being used. There had to be time to be the artist's friend, and there was none.[20]

ANITA GILLETTE

It was true that we didn't have lots of time. But the consolation for me was working with Jack. He came from the theater so he loved to rehearse. The discoveries you made in rehearsals were the most exciting. Jack and I found rewards in rehearsing our scenes together. We also enjoyed a great chemistry that made it a lot of fun.[8]

If Klugman could be irascible with writers, he had a soft spot for actors who made an investment in their work, and he did his best to be supportive.

DON EITNER
(Actor, Multiple Episodes)

> I remember playing the part of a lawyer in an episode entitled "The Hero Syndrome." We were filming a contentious scene where my character was trying to manipulate the situation. I had made some choices as an actor that I thought worked well. However, after we shot the scene, the director wanted to do it over again and change what I did. At that point, Jack stepped in and said, "No, we don't need another take. That was wonderful. I liked what Don did. I think we should keep it." I appreciated the fact that Jack intervened on my behalf, because I too felt the scene worked well as is. It also showed Jack's awareness and generosity in support of another actor.[27]

In the final season (1982-1983), Broadway veteran Anita Gillette joined the cast as Dr. Emily Hanover, an attractive psychiatrist who played an integral part in shows like "Baby Rattlesnakes," "Cry for Help," and "An Act of Violence," which incorporated psychology into the storyline.

    Quincy M.E. needed a spirited female in the show to take some of the burden of being perpetually emphatic off of Quincy.[27]

ANITA GILETTE

> When Jack said that he wanted me to play Emily whom he would eventually marry, I said, "Jack, I

already played your first wife in an earlier episode and I died, remember?" Jack said, "I don't care. When I get married on the show, you're gonna be my wife. If anyone asks, we'll tell them you look a lot like the other wife I had."[8]

Once a show was filmed, there was still a tremendous amount of work to be done in the editing room and subsequent post-production before a final print was sent to the network for broadcast.

JEANENE AMBLER
(Film Editor)

Every day I would get the dailies which was what they shot the day before. My assistant would put them on reels and I would go and look at them in the projection room along with Bill Cairncross (our supervising producer) and the director if he was available.

My assistant would then break the dailies down into rolls, put them up on my bench in the editor's room (lined up according to the script) and I would cut that day's film together. I would run the film through a green machine called the Moviola, with the picture on one side and sound on the other. That enabled me to view and hear everything in sync.

By the end of a six-day shoot, I would hopefully have all but the last day's edited. I'd cut it all together, make sure it looked good, then run a first cut with the director in the screening room. After getting his notes on changes, I'd go back, make those changes, then run the director's cut for Jack and the producer. After any further changes, it was on to post (production) for sound effects, music and dubbing.

Today, the editing process is different. Everything is computerized. The Moviola is a relic of the past. But what a joy it was to run that film through my thumb and forefinger, watching the story unfold as the characters talked to me.[28]

WILLIAM CAIRNCROSS

Once the editing was done, I'd run the show for sound effects. For scenes in the medical examiner's office, I'd spot it for different backgrounds with the various lab instruments, get all the sounds balanced and have them proportionally correct so as not to interfere with the actor's dialog.

If we shot outside and there was interference from traffic noise or airplanes, I'd have the actor come in and loop (rerecord) their lines. Jack wasn't fond of looping, so there were instances where we would put the sound of a show through every filter imaginable and pull out as much dialog as we could.

Later I'd sit in a projection room with the composer and spot music, picking where we felt it should come in. In a dramatic scene, it would enter softly and build, or sometimes come in like a sledgehammer. Once dialog, sound and music was complete, I'd go to the mixing stage and put it all together.[16]

Very seldom were any mistakes made that carried through to a final print sent to the network, but on one occasion it happened.

WILLIAM CAIRNCROSS

We left a guest star's name out of the credits, and found out the night it was to air. So Dick Rabjohn (the film editor) and I ran over to the network, had them shoot the credit on black, took the film down, and spliced it on the bench right there. The technician rewound it, put it up in the telecast magazine and the show went on the air that way. That was a close call and we avoided a major lawsuit.[16]

After seven seasons and 146 episodes, *Quincy* ended production in late March of 1983, and aired its final first run episode on May 11th of that year.

JERI TAYLOR

The gratifying thing about *Quincy* was that it was a show that was about something. I was relatively new when I began writing for the series and it spoiled me for other shows. The satisfaction that a writer gets from writing a show that's substantive, about something important that touches people's lives, was immense. I was proud of doing *Quincy* and I would point with pride to episodes that had a real impact. That was not necessarily the fate of a writer/ producer in episodic television.

I adored Jack. I truly did, because it was apparent from the very beginning that (unlike others that I had worked with), he cared about the quality and excellence of the show. Yes, he could be demanding. But it was not about his ego or his being in the spotlight. The concept for the show being about something came from him. I respected that deeply and missed it in later series I did.[26]

Ironically we never got to know our favorite medical examiner's first name, but we became very well-acquainted and fond of this persistent, contentious, compassionate and caring man who never gave up in his quest to prove his theories, solve his cases, right what was wrong, and make this a better world for all of us!

PHOTO SECTION ONE

Jack Klugman as Quincy: contentious,
compassionate and caring.

Robert Ito (Sam Fujiyama) — dedicated, consistent and reliable.

John S. Ragin (Dr. Robert Astin). As Quincy's superior, he walked a fine line between his administrative responsibilities and keeping his "maverick pathologist" in line.

Bill Stoddard (Craig Stevens) aids Quincy (Jack Klugman) in a desperate search for his kidnapped daughter believed to have been buried alive in "Tissue of Truth," aired October 28, 1977.

Joseph Roman portrayed homicide detective Sgt. Brill who
teamed with Lt. Monahan (Garry Walberg).

Quincy (Jack Klugman) and pathology students Sue (Linda Kelsey) and Hall (Harold Sylvester) dig for bones at a construction site to piece together a 20-year-old murder in "The Thigh Bone's Connected to the Knee Bone." The award-winning 90-minute episode (scripted by producer Lou Shaw) aired February 11, 1977.

Janet Martin (Renne Jarrett) and Robbi Parker (Elizabeth Robinson) ponder their life and death predicament in "Hit and Run At Danny's," telecast March 11, 1977.

Quincy (Jack Klugman) gets reassurance from friend
Danny (Val Bisoglio) in an early episode.

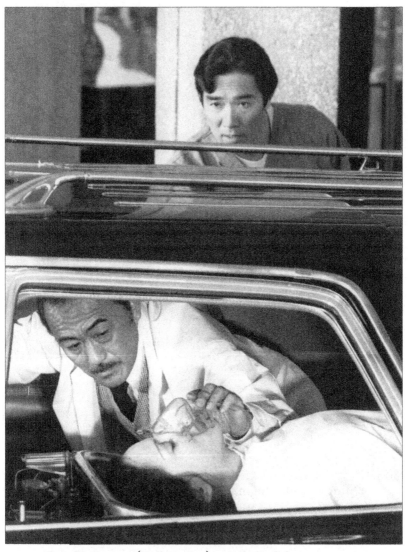

Sam Fujiyama (Robert Ito) watches with concern as
Chief Coroner Hiro (Yuki Shimoda) administers oxygen
to a woman (Louise Sorel) presumed dead from a suicide
try and scheduled for an autopsy in "Has Anybody Here
Seen Quincy?" (Series star Klugman did not appear in
the episode which aired March 18, 1977.)

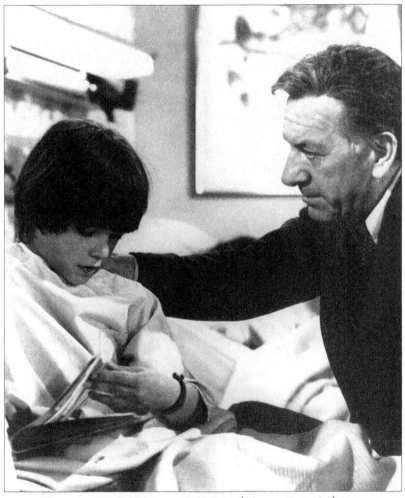

Quincy suspects Joey Harrison (Shane Sinutka) is a
victim of child abuse in "A Good Smack in the Mouth,"
telecast April 15, 1977.

Addie (Melinda Fee) and Arthur Lanz (James Wainwright) are a greedy couple involved in a killing by a lethal dose of radiation in "An Unfriendly Radiance," broadcast April 29, 1977.

Quincy (Jack Klugman) nabs a rapist through lab analysis of evidence gathered from a rape victim in David Moessinger's "Let Me Light the Way." The show was the final one-hour episode of season one (May 27, 1977), and set Klugman on the path of doing more socially relevant storylines.

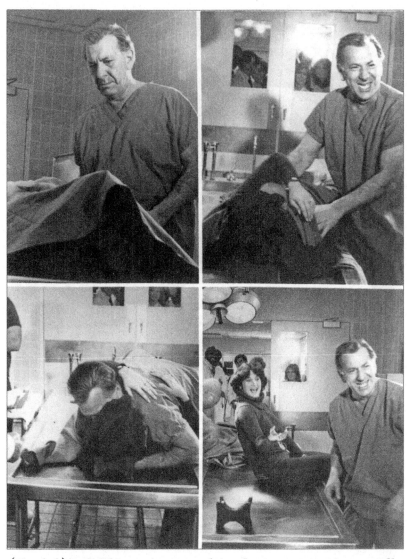

(Top left) Jack Klugman prepared to rehearse a scene supposedly with a dummy under the sheets. (Top right) Klugman discovers the crew has planted a real body — script supervisor Jan Kemper. (Lower left) Klugman gives Kemper a big hug. (Lower right) The series star joins Jan and crew in the laughter.

Quincy (Jack Klugman) suspects that a 140-mph race car crash wasn't the only contributor to the fatality of a former Grand Prix driver in "Speed Trap," from October 5, 1978.

Lloyd Nolan, Jim Rosin, David Hollander and Jack Klugman on the set of "A Test for Living" in June of 1978. Klugman was honored by the Southern California Motion Picture Council for his work on the episode (co-written with Rosin), which concerned the plight of an autistic child.
The show aired October 19, 1978

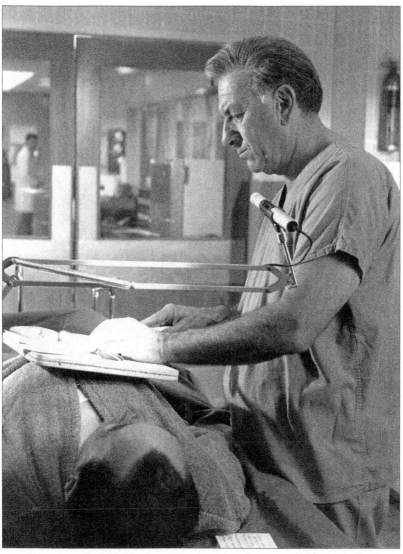

An autopsy on an indigent leads Quincy (Jack Klugman) to
startling conclusions in a drama about an affirmative action
program and malpractice in "Death by Good Intentions,"
telecast October 26, 1978.

Quincy (Jack Klugman) makes sure his tie is straight
before doing a TV interview after a network news anchor
person he confirms has died turns up alive in "Images"
on November 2, 1978.

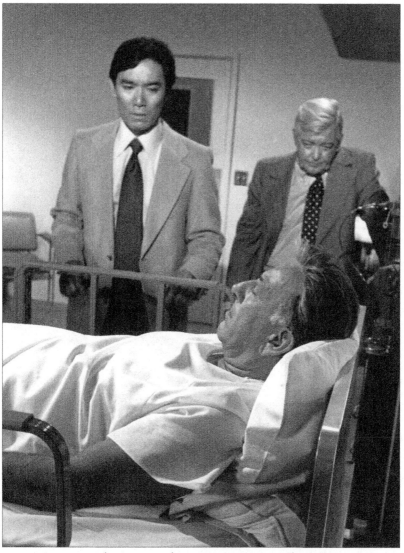

Sam Fujiyama (Robert Ito) and Lt. Monahan (Garry Walberg)
show grave concern as Quincy (Jack Klugman) lies
severely wounded from an errant bullet in
"Even Odds," from November 9, 1978.

Quincy (Jack Klugman) and Sam Fujiyama (Robert Ito) are involved in a search and rescue mission for a seriously injured young man as Bernie (Richard O'Brien) listens intently in "Dead and Alive," written by Jim Rosin, and shown November 16, 1978.

Girlfriend Jenny Drake (Marj Dusay) gives Quincy (Jack Klugman) an adoring look for helping her move into a boarding house where a murder is later discovered. "No Way to Treat a Body" aired November 30, 1978.

Police Lieutenant Monahan (Garry Walberg) testifies at a coroner's inquest looking into the case of an accident victim whose death may have been hastily declared by Quincy in "A Question of Death." Steve Greenberg and Aubrey Solomon's teleplay dealt with legal and medical questions concerning organ transplants and aired January 4, 1979.

Quincy (Jack Klugman) questions a young woman
(Jenny Sherman) when a philandering football star
dies from a virulent strain of VD in "A Small Circle
of Friends," shown January 18, 1979.

An alcoholic doctor (John Dehner) embraces his wife (Anne Francis) after causing a spectacle in a restaurant in "Physician Heal Thyself," telecast February 22, 1979.

Assistant track coach Vic Mascino (Jim Rosin) objects to head
coach Marty O'Banion's (Frank Marth) training of Olympic
hopeful Bobby Nolan (Clark Long) in "The Hope of Elkwood,"
aired December 3, 1980. Michael Braverman's teleplay (from
Rosin's story) examines the consequences of winning at all costs.

Jack Klugman and Jim Rosin on location at College of the
Canyons in Valencia, California, during the filming of "The Hope
of Elkwood," in October 1980.

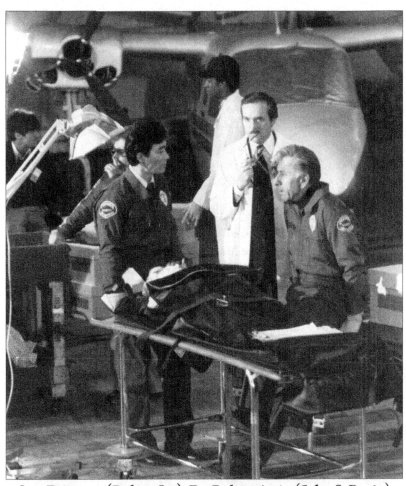

Sam Fujiyama (Robert Ito), Dr. Robert Astin (John S. Ragin) and Quincy (Jack Klugman) in a jetliner crash scene from "Scream to the Skies." Michael Braverman's controversial script examined the lack of safety equipment in airplanes. The show aired February 11, 1980.

Quincy (Jack Klugman) hugs Megan Carmody
(Allison Balson) after aiding the police in her rescue
from a murderous child molester in "Who Speaks for the
Children?", telecast February 25, 1981.

Quincy (Jack Klugman) lends support to a holocaust survivor (Martin Balsam) brought into court by a neo-Nazi on slander charges in Sam Egan's drama "Stolen Tears," March 17, 1982.

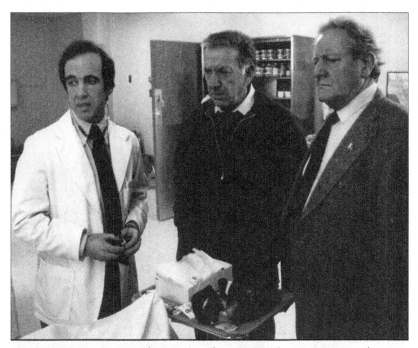

Dr. Marty Rothman (Jim Rosin), Quincy (Jack Klugman) and
Sgt. Wendorf (Henry Beckman) are concerned for Ginger Reeves
(Kelly Preston) in a coma after ingesting alcohol and drugs. "On
Dying High" aired February 9, 1983 and dealt with the
hypocrisy and widespread acceptance of alcohol and drug use.

Quincy (Jack Klugman) surrenders his longtime
bachelorhood and weds Dr. Emily Hanover (Anita Gillette)
after a stormy courtship in "Quincy's Wedding, Part II," the
conclusion of a two-part episode on February 23, 1983.
The two-parter was scripted by producer Jeri Taylor and
directed by executive producer David Moessinger.

QUINCY M.E.

(1976-1983)

Broadcast History

October 1976 – January 1977 – NBC – Sunday 9:30-11:00 pm
February 1977 – May 1977 – NBC – Friday 10:00-11:00 pm
June 1977 – July 1977 – NBC – Friday 9:30-11:00 pm
July 1977 – August 1978 – NBC – Friday 10:00-11:00 pm
September 1978 – April 1980 – NBC – Thursday 9:00-10:00 pm
April 1980 – June 1983 – NBC – Wednesday 10:00-11:00 pm
June 1983 – September 1983 – NBC – Saturday 9:00-10:00 pm

The Cast

Dr. R. Quincy . . . . Jack Klugman (1976 –1983)

Sam Fujiyama . . . . Robert Ito (1976 –1983)

Dr. Robert Astin . . . . John S. Ragin (1976 –1983)

Lt. Frank Monahan . . . . Garry Walberg (1976 –1983)

Danny Tovo . . . . Val Bisoglio (1976 –1983)

Sgt. Brill. . . . . Joseph Roman (1976 –1983)

Eddie (Forensic Photographer) . . . . Eddie Garrett (1976 –1983)

Lee Potter. . . . . Lynette Mettey (1976 –1977)

Dr. Emily Hanover . . . . Anita Gillette (1982 –1983)

Marc (Lab Technician) . . . . . . Marc Scott Taylor (1978 –1982)

Diane (The Waitress) . . . . Diane Markoff (1978–1983)

John (The Bartender) . . . . John Nolan (1977–1983)

Jim Barnes (Assistant D.A.) . . . . James Watson, Jr. (1978–1982)

Robin Rollin (Astin's Secretary). . . . Karen Philipp (1978–1979)

Jeff Sellers (Lab Technician) . . . . . . Jonathan Segal (1977–1978)

QUINCY M.E.

Season One

(1976 –1977)

Episode Titles	Air Dates

Episodes 1-6 (Program length following title)

1. Go Fight City Hall – To the Death! (90 minutes) 10/3/1976
2. Who's Who in Neverland (90 minutes) 10/10/1976
3. A Star is Dead (90 minutes) 11/28/1976
4. Hot Ice, Cold Hearts (90 minutes) 1/2/1977
5. Snake Eyes (Two hours) 2/4/1977
6. The Thigh Bone's Connected to the
   Knee Bone (90 minutes) 2/11/1977

Episodes 7-16 (All one hour duration)

7. Visitors in Paradise 2/18/1977
8. The Two Sides of Truth 2/25/1977
9. Hit and Run at Danny's 3/11/1977
10. Has Anybody Here Seen Quincy? 3/18/1977
11. A Good Smack in the Mouth 4/15/1977
12. The Hot Dog Murder 4/22/1977
13. An Unfriendly Radiance 4/29/1977
14. Sullied Be Thy Name 5/6/1977
15. Valleyview 5/13/1977
16. Let Me Light the Way 5/27/1977

#1. Go Fight City Hall – To the Death!
Written by: Lou Shaw and Glen Larson
Directed by: E. W. Swackhamer

A secretary in the Deputy Mayor's office is found strangled on the beach. The police arrest a young drifter whom they find nearby with her purse. Quincy believes the suspect is innocent, and when the city controller is found dead, the persistent medical examiner uncovers a conspiracy behind both deaths.

Hari Rhodes (Deputy Mayor Collins), Denny Miller (Ben Chase), Henry Darrow (Dr. Rivera), George Wyner (Marcos), Woodrow Parfrey (Bower), Dimitra Arliss (Shirley), Ric Podell (Peter Gordon), Fay DeWitt (Nurse Audrey), Marjorie Battles (Marilyn), John Furlong (First Reporter), Jerry Daniels (Second Reporter), Martha Smith (Diane Johnson), James Rosin (Police Officer).

#2. Who's Who in Neverland?
Teleplay by: Michael Kozoll and Richard M. Powell
Story by: Richard M. Powell
Directed by Steven H. Stern

A wealthy woman writing a tell-all book about some important people is found dead in a motel room without identification. Her body is brought to the medical examiner's office where she is thought to be a prostitute who died from cirrhosis. Then Quincy finds some inconsistencies in her blood work which may be linked to the death of her literary agent who died from the same condition.

Dina Merrill (Claire Garner), Carol Lynley (Lynn Dressler), Monte Markham (Harold Fredericks), Phyllis Newman (Mrs. Ellis), Joanna Barnes (Margo Bentley), Fred Sadoff (Arthur Ellis), Andy Romano

(Derrick Kendel), Sheilah Wells (Secretary), Jan Shuter (Lorraine), Richard Libertini (Felsenfield), Jim Boles (Gus).

#3. A Star is Dead
Written by: Lou Shaw, Michael Kozoll and Glen Larson
Directed by: Noel Black

A well known movie star is found dead in her bedroom, of an apparent suicide. Then a scandal sheet publisher suggests that Congressman Charles Sinclair (a friend of Quincy) may be implicated in her death.

Robert Foxworth (Sinclair), William Daniels (Paul Reardon), Donna Mills (Roberta Rhodes), June Lockhart (Mrs. Rhodes), Frank Marth (Roy Keefer), Peter Palmer (Lance Tucker), Dick Wesson (Clarence), H.M. Wynant (Doyle), Carla Borelli (Danielle).

#4. Hot Ice, Cold Hearts
Written by: Sean Baine
Directed by: Bruce Kessler

A quiet weekend for Quincy and girlfriend Lee Potter on Catalina Island is disrupted when Quincy becomes involved in the rescue of a young diver retrieved from the water. It appears he was stung by a venomous stone fish not found locally, and deliberately poisoned.

Stuart Whitman (Sheriff Parsons), Robert Alda (Professor Wren), Fernando Lamas (Moreno), Andrew Prine (Alex Kale), Mariana Hill (Lisa).

#5. Snake Eyes
Teleplay by: Joel Oliansky and Michael Sloan
Story by: Lou Shaw
Directed by: Joel Oliansky

While in Lake Tahoe for a forensic pathologist convention, Quincy (accompanied by Lee and Danny) finds the guests and staff at their hotel stricken with a mysterious illness. Quincy and several colleagues are unable to find the cause. At the same time the hotel owner plays down the situation, concerned it will affect business. When the ill victims don't improve and several deaths occur, terrified guests begin to panic. Yet allowing them to leave could spread the disease.

Van Johnson (Al Ringerman), Frank Converse (Dr. Larry Pine), Jo Ann Pflug (Mrs. Pine), Buddy Hackett (Ronnie Fletcher), Val Avery (Rawley Dinehart), Milt Kamen (Leo Burke), Joey Foreman (Marv Bracken), Frank Maxwell (Dr. Michaels), William Mims (Dr. Groot), Michele Roman (Angie).

#6. The Thigh Bone's Connected to the Knee Bone
Teleplay by: Lou Shaw
Story by: Lou Shaw and Tony Lawrence
Directed: Alex March

A human thigh bone is discovered at a building construction site. Quincy and a group of pathology students he's teaching reconstruct a human identity from the single bone which reopens a twenty-year-old murder case and ultimately brings about a confrontation between Quincy and the killer.

Stephen Macht (Frank Halley), Linda Kelsey (Sue), Elisha Cook,

Jr. (Charles Trout), Fred Grandy (Milt Jordan), Harold Sylvester (Hall), John Davis Chandler (Robert Gideon), Ron Thompson (Claude Stern), Gus Corrado (Fred Burton).

#7. Visitors in Paradise
Written by: Michael Sloan
Directed by: Ivan Dixon

Quincy and Danny take a fishing trip to the town of Paradise. Once they arrive, a woman asks Quincy to reopen a case involving her mother's death. However, once he agrees to look into the matter, the M.E. is threatened by one of the local residents.

Jack Kelly (Peter Devlin), Pernell Roberts (Sheriff Connelly), Hilary Thompson (Jessica Casey), Roger Davis (Paul Taggart), William Sylvester (Joe Crawford), Ivor Francis (Garfield), Stanley Kamel (Cullis), Barry Cahill (John Casey), Jamie Lee Curtis (Girl), Peter Virgo (Man at Store).

#8. The Two Sides of Truth
Written by: Eugene Thompson
Directed by: Ron Satlof

Quincy is opposed in court by his mentor Dr. Herbert Stone, the top pathology expert in the country, in a case involving homicide and insurance fraud.

Barry Sullivan (Dr. Herbert Stone), Mark Goddard (Martin Borland), Michael Callan (William Farrell), Suzanne Rogers (Elaine Farrell), Frank Campanella (Max Wilbur), Jason Wingreen (Dr. Freeman), June Dayton (Judge), Aimeé Eccles (Alice Ting).

#9. Hit and Run at Danny's
Written by: Gregory Dinallo
Directed by: Alvin Ganzer

Danny faces possible closure for allowing Robbi Parker to leave his bar intoxicated — she's been found dead in her car after a hit-and-run accident. Attempting to help his friend, Quincy discovers Parker had extensive plastic surgery to change her identify, her plastic surgeon is reluctant to discuss her, and then he finds the government is involved.

Carl Betz (Paul Barkley), Renne Jarrett (Janet Marth), Joe Maross (John Blake), Jack Colvin (Legget), Elizabeth Robinson (Robbi Parker), Than Wyenn (Dr. Redman), H.M. Wynant (Maxwell), Jan Shutan (Ginny), Clyde Kusatsu (Hokaido), Chanin Hale (Woman).

#10. Has Anybody Here Seen Quincy?
Written by: Michael Sloan and Glen Larson
Directed by: Steven H. Stern

Quincy is nowhere to be found and the medical examiner's office is in chaos. Enter Dr. Hiro, the celebrated pathologist who finds that a woman about to be autopsied is actually still alive.

Yuki Shimoda (Dr. Hiro), Louise Sorel (Harriet Crawford), Kelly Jean Peters (Charlene Taylor), Stu Gilliam (Dr. Hiro's Driver), Bob Crane (Dr. Jamison), Stewart Moss (Jack Taylor), Paul Lambert (Jack Wilson), Jesse White (Rental Car Agent), Nancy Fox (Sally Frier).

#11. A Good Smack in the Mouth
Teleplay by: Gregory Dinallo
Story by: Glen Larson and Jack Klugman
Directed by: Jackie Cooper

Quincy examines young Joey Harrison after a car accident and finds evidence of child abuse. Based on the child's behavior, Quincy believes his mother to be responsible and suggests the father take Joey on a fishing trip while he convinces the mother to seek help. Then Quincy finds out he may have given Joey to the real abuser.

Allen Case (Stuart Harrison), Colin Wilcox (Martha Harrison), Shane Sinutko (Joey), Barbara Babcock (Melissa Astin), Dabney Coleman (Dr. Burt Travers), Monica Lewis (Mona Duffy), Gloria DeHaven (Doreen), Gregg Palmer (Sean Duffy), Patricia Joyce (Dr. Laura Kaplan).

#12. The Hot Dog Murder
Written by: B.W. Sandefur
Directed by: Alex March

A medical student asks Quincy to investigate the death of a prison inmate who supposedly choked to death on a hot dog but may have been murdered.

William Windom (Arthur Brandise), Marianne McAndrew (Dolores), Joshua Shelley (Whitley), Claire Brennan (Sara), Wynn Irwin (Levine), William Swan (Dr. Sharp).

#13. An Unfriendly Radiance
Written by: Rudolph Borchert
Directed by: Corey Allen

An ex-con is accused of manslaughter in the death of a nuclear worker, but Quincy's autopsy shows the man may have died from a lethal dose of radiation.

James Wainwright (Arthur Lanz), Melinda Fee (Addie), Jerry Douglas (Johnson), Joby Baker (Donald Bigelow), Ronald Joseph (Ray Sanchez), Carmine Caridi (Dr. Brown), Edith Diaz (Maria Sanchez), Casey Kasem (Sy Wallace).

#14. Sullied Be Thy Name
Teleplay by: Gregory Dinallo and Irving Pearlberg
Story by: Gregory Dinallo
Directed by: Jackie Cooper

Father Terrell, a close friend of Lt. Monahan and a well-known crusader against pornography, is found dead in the room of a high-class prostitute.

John Saxon (Carlo Dicassa), E.J. Peaker (Michelle Rowan), Linden Chiles (Monsignor), Joseph Campanella (Jules Draper), Caroline McWilliams (Beverly Conrad), Eddie Firestone (Thayler).

#15. Valleyview
Teleplay by: Susan Woodley and Irving Pearlberg
Story by: Susan Woodley
Directed by: Ron Satlof

When several people die mysteriously at Valleyview, a convalescent home, Quincy believes someone may be performing "mercy killings."

Robert Webber (Dr. John Franklin), Carolyn Jones (Nurse Grayson), Christopher Connelly (Paul Colby), Jason Evers (Dr. Peter James), Anthony Eisley (Mr. Schroeder).

#16. Let Me Light the Way
Teleplay by: David Moessinger
Story by: Carol Saraceno and David Moessinger
Directed by: David Moessinger

When emergency room personnel wash a rape victim and discard her clothing, Quincy is unable to collect evidence against a suspected rapist. Then rape counselor Carol Bowen, who tries to aid Quincy and Sam, becomes the next victim.

Adrienne Barbeau (Carol Bowen), John Ireland (Jack Pacard), Luke Askew (Carl DeReatis), Henry Beckman (Bellwood), Kim Cattrall (Joy DeReatis), Barbara Collentine (Fay Willard), Regis Cordic (Judge), Judy Farrell (Louise Porter), George Wyner (Richard Feldman).

QUINCY M.E.

Season Two

(1977-1978)

Episode Titles	Air Dates
17. No Deadly Secret	9/16/1977
18. A Blow to the Head – A Blow to the Heart	9/23/1977
19. A Dead Man's Truth	9/30/1977
20. A Question of Time	10/14/1977
21. Death Casts a Vote	10/21/1977
22. Tissue of Truth	10/28/1977
23. Holding Pattern	11/4/1977
24. Main Man	11/11/1977
25. The Hero Syndrome	11/18/1977
26. Touch of Death	12/2/1977
27. The Deadly Connection	12/9/1977
28. Last of the Dinosaurs	12/16/1977
29. Crib Job	1/6/1978
30. Matters of Life & Death	1/20/1978
31. Passing	1/27/1978
32. Accomplice to Murder	2/3/1978
33. Ashes to Ashes	2/10/1978
34. Gone But Not Forgotten	2/17/1978
35. Double Death	3/3/1978
36. Requiem for the Living	3/10/1978

#17. No Deadly Secret
Written by: Wallace Ware
Directed by: Jackie Cooper

After Quincy performs an autopsy on an injured man who died on his boat, the body, autopsy report and the night worker who witnessed the procedure mysteriously disappear.

Ina Balin (Stella Ross), Keene Curtis (Forsythe), Norman Burton (Max), Elaine Joyce (Irene), Paul Mantee (Carl Hopwood), Dennis Burkley (Tom Tom), Harry Landers (Hughes), Ben Frank (Coolidge), Susan Tolsky (Chemist).

#18. A Blow to the Head, A Blow to the Heart
Written by: Mann Rubin
Directed by: Corey Allen

When a boxer dies after a bout, his wife believes it wasn't caused from the blows in the ring, and she asks Quincy to perform an autopsy.

Moses Gunn (Ben McDade), Nehemiah Persoff (Matt Dorsey), Lynne Moody (Laura Stokes), Gloria Manon (Jill), Norman Alden, Joe Louis as himself.

#19. A Dead Man's Truth
Written by: Adrian Leeds
Directed by: Vic Morrow

A rookie police officer shoots a burglar and his explanation of what happened doesn't match Quincy's findings.

Dabney Coleman (Officer Peter O'Neil), David Spielberg (Officer

James Wells), Howard Hesseman (D.A.), Nora Heflin (Charlotte), Mark Lambert (Denis Dobbs), Joseph Gallison (Director).

#20. A Question of Time
Written by: Irving Pearlberg
Directed by: Ray Danton

An attorney interferes with Quincy's investigation of an alleged accidental drowning at a health spa.

Peter Mark Richman (Walter Kingman), Rudy Solari (Bridges), Brenda Scott (Mrs. Holloway), John Alderson (Holloway), Peter Hobbs (Dr. Benton), Mike Lane (Rossi), Irene Tedrow (Dr. Ruth Thaler).

#21. Death Casts a Vote
Written by: William Froug
Directed by: Ron Satlof

Two opposing labor leaders battling for votes come under suspicion when Quincy believes the alleged suicide of a young farm worker appears to be murder.

James Gregory (Tony Gordon), Robert F. Simon (Mr. Brady), Ronald G. Joseph (Luis), Jerome Thor (Lynch).

#22. Tissue of Truth
Written by: Max McClellan
Directed by: Ray Danton

When an abductor is killed, a half-eaten apple is the only clue to the location of a kidnapped teenager buried alive with a limited supply of oxygen.

Craig Stevens (Bill Stoddard), Lenka Peterson (Amanda Stoddard), Ivor Francis (Mr. Ambrose), Jonathan Segal (Jeff Sellers), Ralph Taeger (Kinny), Royal Dano (Holsang), Timothy Blake (Miss Gloria).

#23. Holding Pattern
Teleplay by: Robert Hammer
Story by: Adam Singer
Directed by: Ron Satlof

A deadly virus threatens terrorists and passengers aboard a hijacked airliner.

Gerald S. O'Loughlin (Adam Fielding), Christine Belford (Sonya), Robert Viharo (Hijacker), Phil Leeds (Fishman), John McKinney (Pilot), Peggy Crosby (Girl), Bonnie Johns (Anne Wilson), Madison Mason (LAX Official), Dan Meehan (Dr. Halbertson).

#24. Main Man
Teleplay by: Irving Pearlberg
Story by: Ray Danton
Directed by: Ray Danton

A congenital brain defect might kill a high school athlete if he continues playing football, but the boy's father and the school seem more concerned with winning.

Eugene Roche (Walter Daniels), Peter Brown (Coach), Scott Colomby (Steve Daniels), Julie Adams (Mrs. Daniels), Laurence Haddon (Spalding), Byron Webster (Griswold), Joe George

(Thomas).

#25. The Hero Syndrome
Written by: Albert Aley
Directed by: Gerald Mayer

A longshoreman confesses to killing a hated loan shark, but Quincy is not convinced of his guilt.

Robert Walker Jr. (Peter Thorwall), Shelly Novack (Ben), Carmine Caridi (Rocco), Judson Pratt (Antrim), Roy Jordan (Hennafy), Don Eitner (Tyler), Maxine Stuart (Judge Daley), Candy Castillo (Vietnam Vet).

#26. Touch of Death
Written by: Joe Hyams and Pat Strong
Directed by: Alexander Singer

Sam Fujiyama quits the Medical Examiner's office when Quincy violates his cultural tradition by performing an autopsy on a Japanese martial arts movie star.

Keye Luke (Hitoshi Hiyato), Mako (Mr. Yamaguchi), Joanna Kerns (Lily), Booth Coleman (Dr. Edwards), Harold Sakata (Sensei).

#27. The Deadly Connection
Written by: Sheldon Stark
Directed by: Alex March

In a small ranching community, Quincy and Sam search for an unidentified ailment that is killing cattle and affecting local residents.

Lonny Chapman (Paul Davis), Elisha Cook, Jr. (Henry Davis), Guy Stockwell (Jack Porter), Gil Sarna (Gutierrez).

#28. Last of the Dinosaurs
Written by: Leonard Stadd
Directed by: Ray Danton

Quincy and Lt. Monahan clash over the actual cause of death to Western movie star Will Preston.

Cameron Mitchell (Dan Granger), John Anderson (Movie Director), Carolyn Jones (Sylvia Preston), Kario Salem (Mel), Marianne Bunch (Betty), Christopher Pitney (Nick), Art Lewis (Freddy).

#29. Crib Death
Written by: Milton Gelman
Directed by: Alex March

Quincy agrees to help a friend who runs a program for teens and senior citizens. The program is in jeopardy because a teen member is accused of killing an elderly man.

Rosey Grier as himself, Milton Selzer (Mr. Avery), Frank Faylen (Mr. Chanoose), Todd Davis (Victor Garn), J. Pat O'Malley (Mr. Brannigan), Read Morgan (Brownie), T.K. Carter (Mojo).

#30. Matters of Life and Death
Written by: Albert Aley
Directed by: Paul Krasny

Quincy becomes involved in a case of medical negligence while filling in for a doctor in a small California community.

Henry Beckman (Police Chief Hartman), Walter Brooke (Dr. Gilliam), Louise Latham (Nurse Katherine Lowry), John Fiedler (Howard Clausen), Jim Antonio), (Dr. George Bristol), Hoke Howell (Bud Cowley), Sarah Rush (Trish Granby), Natalie Trundy (Myra Hammond), Argentina Brunetti (Mrs. Maggiore).

#31. Passing
Teleplay by: Mann Rubin and Samuel Shamforoff
Story by: Mann Rubin and Lois Gibson
Directed by: David Alexander

A skull may be the key to a labor leader's disappearance and a mobster's subsequent rise to power.

Simon Oakland (Sal Jarrett), Zohra Lampert (Lynn Peters), Sondra Blake (Megan Molloy), Neva Patterson (Mrs. Lockwood), Michael Strong (Mob Boss), Phillip Pine (Brown), Jonathan Segal (Jeff Sellers), Frank Maxwell (Ross Brickner).

#32. Accomplice to Murder
Written by: Frank Telford
Directed by: Paul Krasny

A burglar is accused of killing a woman, but Quincy believes she died from prior blows inflicted by her influential husband.

Belinda Montgomery (Bonnie DeMarco), Robert Colbert (William Steele), Joe E. Tata (Tony DeMarco), Byron Morrow (Downing), Ford Rainey (Doctor Bellamy), T.J. Castranova (Officer Harris). James Rosin (Officer Jay Klein), Lew Brown (Judge Erickson),

Anne Newman-Mantee (Esther Kellogg), Randy Stumpf (Joey Kling), Chevi Colton (Mrs. Hayes), Karen Phillipp (Martha Steele).

#33. Ashes to Ashes
Teleplay by: Max Hodge
Story by: Charles McDaniel
Directed by: Herb Wallerstein

A businessman's wife dies in a bar from an apparent heart attack, but Quincy suspects foul play and that her husband may have been involved.

John Fink (Richard Yager), Judith Baldwin (Marie Yager), Simone Griffeth (Cindy Allen), Larry D. Mann (Dr. Jones), Pitt Herbert (Dr. Gehringer).

#34. Gone But Not Forgotten
Written by: Tom Sawyer and Reyn Parke
Directed by: Paul Krasny

A newspaper editor joins Quincy to look into the murder of an eccentric inventor whose residence included a supposedly impenetrable security system.

Joan Van Ark (Bert Phillips), Ramon Bieri (Ben Mular), John

Colicos (Harlan Standish), Patricia Smith (Julia Fairchild), Nate
Esformes (George Mendes), Sidney Clute (Harry).

#35. Double Death
Written by: Albert Aley
Directed by: Robert Douglas

Quincy tries to clear Dr. Astin's name in the rushed autopsy of a
nightclub owner killed in a fire.

George Wyner (Mr. Glendon), Lara Parker (Miss Wilson), Leonard
Frey (Mr. Bristol), Frank Campanella (Carl), Bob Hastings (Judge
Whelan), Jonathan Segal (Jeff), Joseph Perry (Solly), Olan Soule
(Mortician), Peggy Crosby (Waitress).

$36. Requiem for the Living
Teleplay by: Irving Pearlberg
Story by: Ray Danton
Directed by: Rowe Wallerstein

Quincy and Sam are held hostage by a poisoned mobster who
commands them to find out how he was poisoned before he dies so
he can identify the person responsible and enact his revenge.

John Vernon (Vincent DiNardi), Val Avery (Carlo), Ina Balin
(Irene), Max Showalter (Doctor), Larry Gelman (Rossiani), Peter
Virgo (1ˢᵗ Hood), Ben Marino (2ⁿᵈ Hood), Henry Slate (3ʳᵈ Hood),
Peggy Crosby (Dee Dee), Terri Lynn Wood (Lisa).

QUINCY M.E.

Season Three
(1978 –1979)

Episode Titles	Air Dates
37. The Last Six Hours	9/21/1978
38. Speed Trap	10/12/1978
39. A Test for Living	10/19/1978
40. Death by Good Intensions	10/26/1978
41. Images	11/2/1978
42. Even Odds	11/9/1978
43. Dead and Alive	11/16/1978
44. No Way to Treat a Body	11/30/1978
45. A Night to Raise the Dead	12/7/1978
46. A Question of Death	1/4/1979
47. House of No Return	1/11/1979
48. A Small Circle of Friends	1/18/1979
49. The Depth of Beauty	1/25/1979
50. Walk Softly Through the Night (two hours)	2/1/1979
51. Aftermath	2/8/1979
52. Dark Angel	2/15/1979
53. Physician Heal Thyself	2/22/1979
54. Promises to Keep	3/1/1979

#37. The Last Six Hours
Written by: Steven Greenberg and Aubrey Solomon
Directed by: Corey Allen

Quincy finds himself in a desperate race to isolate a mysterious poison that has already claimed two lives and poses a deadly threat to Sam Fujiyama.

Sharon Acker (Barbara), John Anderson (Dr. DeWile), Scott Marlowe (Dicenzio), Paul Mantee (Foreman), Steve Franken (Dr. Kitei), Karen Philipp (Secretary), Len Lesser (DeGroot), Paul Carr (Dr. Weiss).

#38. Speed Trap
Teleplay by: Steven Greenberg and Aubrey Solomon
Directed by: Ron Satlof

Quincy suspects that a 140-mph race car crash wasn't the only contributor to the fatality of a former Grand Prix driver.

Simon Oakland (Chuck Thomas), Phillip R. Allen (Dr. Finley), Erica Hagen (Sherry Bannon), Michael Delano (Mark Hellman), Cassie Yates (Judy Fellner), Frank Parker (Dr. Weiss).

#39. A Test for Living
Teleplay by: Jack Klugman, James Rosin and Patrick Mathews
Story by: Jack Klugman
Directed by: Ron Satlof

Quincy becomes personally involved in the case of Timmy Carson, a child recently diagnosed as autistic by his friend, psychiatrist Herb Shuman. Treatment is available at a special school, but to get Timmy enrolled, Shuman and Quincy face a two-front campaign. On the one hand, they must convince the school's administrators that Timmy is in fact autistic, not mentally challenged as they believe. On the other, they must convince Timmy's parents that the expense would be worthwhile. Having suffered much, they are deeply pessimistic about their son's future.

Lloyd Nolan (Dr. Shuman), Sam Groom (David Carson), Kelly Jean Peters (Mary Carson), David Hollander (Timmy), Tracey Gold (Lisa), Philip Abbott (Elliot Phillips), Henry Jones (Austin Barnes), Susan Gay Powell (Dr. Laura Green), William Mims (Dr. Blenham), James Rosin (Ward Attendant), Eugene Glazer (Officer Keefer), Rolly Fanton (Neighbor), Cecil Reddick (Waiter).

#40. Death by Good Intentions
Teleplay by: Robert Crais
Story by: Howard Dimsdale and Michael Halperin
Directed by: Ron Satlof

A young Afro-American doctor's alleged incompetence poses a threat to a hospital's affirmative-action program unless Quincy can prove that the physician's patient was murdered.

Brock Peters (Dr. Frank Mathews), Roger Robinson (Dr. Eric Taylor), Pernell Roberts (Dr. Chester Banning), Hari Rhodes (Dr. Phillip Moran), Elsa Raven (Nurse Davenport), Robert Doqui (Dr. Charles), Ken Martinez (Dr. Perez), George Deloy (Jerry Bremmer).

#41. Images

Teleplay by: Aubrey Solomon and Steve Greenberg
Story by: Ray Danton
Directed by: Ray Danton

Quincy is fired by Astin when he persists in a bizarre theory that a TV network newswoman is dead and her murderer has assumed her identity.

Jessica Walters (Jessica Ross), Whit Bissell (Dr. Thornton), Jack Hogan (Ron Gordon), Robert Ellenstein (Bert), Peggy McCay (Nun), James Watson, Jr. (Asst. D.A. Barnes), Karen Philipp (Robin).

#42. Even Odds

Written by: Pamela Glasser
Directed by: Ray Danton

Quincy lies near death, the victim of a gunman's bullet, while Lt. Monahan, Dr. Astin and Sam Fujiyama attempt to solve a robbery-homicide by applying techniques taught to them by the medical examiner in previous cases.

Edward Grover (Dr. Monroe), Richard McKenzie (John Holmes), Dennis Madalone (Richard Billings), Eileen Barnett (Sharon Jordan), Sam Cotton (Jim Jordan), Angelina Estrada (Mrs. Herrera).

#43. Dead and Alive
Written by: James Rosin
Directed by: Jim Benson

Peter Neilson, an apparent victim in a fiery crash, becomes the object of Quincy's thorough identification process. But Neilson's mother and sister insist that he's still alive, based on cryptic phone calls from a person claiming to be Peter.

Priscilla Pointer (Sarah Neilson), Ayn Ruymen (Carol), Frank Marth (George Stanton), Harry Townes (Dr. Reisman), Harry Landers (Riordan), Nicholas Georgiade (Andros), David Hurst (Dr. Webber), Sheila Larken (Dr. Linda Redman), Richard O'Brien (Bernie), Howard Dayton (Charlie), Karen Philipp (Robin).

#44. No Way to Treat a Body
Written by: Robert Crais and Bill Seal
Directed by: Ron Satlof

The bizarre discovery of four mummified women, one of them a murder victim, pits Quincy against a boarding house of off-beat characters.

Bibi Osterwald (Rose Kaufman), Malcolm Atterbury (Raymond), Ed Begley, Jr. (Speed), Wallace Rooney (Professor), Al Checco (Max), David Ralphe (Dr. Ellis), Marj Dusay (Jenny).

#45. A Night to Raise the Dead
Teleplay by: Michael Halperin
Story by: Peter Thompson
Directed by: Gene Nelson

Quincy fights political corruption to prevent a potential typhoid outbreak caused by diseased bodies unleashed from a hillside cemetery during a torrential rainstorm.

Greg Morris (Clifford Collier), Robert Sampson (David Brady), Kevin Hagen (Dr. Albers), Jackie Joseph (Claudia Turner), Frank Aletter (Alan Turner), Henry Slate (Foreman).

#46. A Question of Death
Teleplay by: Aubrey Solomon and Steve Greenberg
Story by: Peter Thompson, Robert Crais, Aubrey Solomon and Steve Greenberg
Directed by: Ran Danton

Quincy is slapped with a multi-million dollar malpractice suit when he signs a kidney transplant order on an accident victim who allegedly is not yet dead.

Granville VanDusen (Raymond Morrison), Edward Grover (Dr. Monroe), Kenneth O'Brien (Andy Corey), Peter Hobbs (Dr. Peterson), Royal Dano (Dr. Williams), Helen Funai (Dr. Helen Matsuro), Don Keefer (Terrence Morgan).

#47. House of No Return
Teleplay by: Aubrey Solomon and Steve Greenberg
Story by: Deborah Klugman and Steve Greenberg
Directed by: Harvey Laidman

Quincy goes undercover at a county institute for the criminally insane to substantiate murder and patient abuse charges made by a dead inmate's mother.

James McEachin (Dr. Richard Maxwell), Alex Henteloff (Bill Carruthers), David Hooks (Dr. Henry Morris), Hank Brandt (Herb Saunders), Joseph Ruskin (Rollins), Virginia Capers (Emily Barwell), Art Aragon (Maxie), Tony Brubaker (Jo Barwell).

#48. A Small Circle of Friends
Teleplay by: Steve Greenberg and Aubrey Solomon
Story by: Jack Morton, Steve Greenberg and Aubrey Solomon
Directed by: Peter Thompson

Venereal disease threatens to erupt into an epidemic unless Quincy can find a prostitute suspected as the source.

James Keach (Gary Harlan), Jo Ann Pflug (Marsha), Raymond St. Jacques (Dr. Martin), Jenny Sherman (Gabrielle Martin), Kathryn Leigh Scott (Laura Ramsey), Cecilia Hart (Jackie), Shawn Michaels (Mr. Johnson), Lee Paul (Joe Ramsey).

#49. The Depth of Beauty
Teleplay by: Robert Crais
Story by: Robert Crais and Barbara Evans
Directed by: Ray Danton

A negligent plastic surgeon becomes the target of Quincy's crusade to end the doctor's disfigurement of innocent victims.

Jane Greer (Dorrie Larken), Donald May (Dr. Walt Mitchell), Garnett Smith (Dr. Emil Green), Ryan MacDonald (Ed Connors), Walter Brooke (Harry Chase), Joey Foreman (Ed Carlton), Leonard Stone (Judge Monroe).

#50. Walk Softly Through the Night (Two Hours)
Written by: David Moessinger
Directed by: Paul Krasny

When the son of a friend dies of a drug overdose, Quincy teams up with a pre-med student to find the source of the illicit narcotics and stop the trafficking on campus.

Michael Constantine (Brock Campbell), A Martinez (Marty Herrera), Charles Aidman (Dr. Mason Collela), James A. Watson (Asst. D.A. Barnes), William Prince (Prosecutor), Dimitra Arliss (Dr. Kirschner), Yale Summers (Coroner), Tom Williams (Director), Peggy Walton Walker (Lisa), Alan Manson (Norm Hulzer).

#51. Aftermath
Teleplay by: Steven Greenberg and Aubrey Solomon
Story by: Peter Thompson
Directed by: Tony Mordente

In the wake of one of the nation's worst airline disasters, Quincy suspects that an ingenious form of sabotage may have caused the crash.

John Larch (Riggins), George Gaynes (Banning), Burr DeBenning (Wilson), Rod Colbin (Myers), Pat Smith (Mrs. Myers).

#52. Dark Angel
Written by: Robert Crais
Directed by: Ray Danton

Quincy must battle his own suspicions and mounting political pressure to try to clear a veteran police officer accused of killing a drug-crazed teenager.

Neville Brand (Bates), William Daniels (Trusdale), Michael D. Roberts (Waters), Robert Stanley (Tony), Michael Horton (Steve), Marshall Thompson (Mr. Harris), Stack Pierce (Murray), Bill Zuckert (Commissioner).

#53. Physician Heal Thyself
Written by: Aubrey Solomon and Steve Greenberg
Directed by: Corey Allen

When a teenage girl dies as a result of a botched abortion, Quincy discovers a conspiracy of silence among medical men in protecting the guilty surgeon.

John Dehner (Dr. Shafer), Anne Francis (Mrs. Shafer), June
Lockhart (Dr. Blair), Asher Brauner (Dr. Tompkins), Joby Baker
(Ken Jackson), James Rosin (Jeff Price), Virginia Vincent (Mrs.
Reed), Tara Buckman (Julie Reed), Phillip Pine (Belden), Milt
Kogan (Dr. Taylor).

#54. Promises to Keep
Teleplay by: Erich Collier
Directed by: Harvey Laidman

Quincy's decision to remarry forces him to question his obsession
with work when he emotionally relives the tragic days leading up to
the death of his beloved first wife.

Anita Gillette (Helen Quincy), Sharon Acker (Lynn Montgomery),
Lonny Chapman (Dr. Jim Jordan), Shannon Farnon (Mrs.
Thatcher).

#55. Semper-Fidelis
Teleplay by: Robert Crais
Story by: Maurice Klugman
Directed by: Tony Mordente

A shocking surprise awaits Quincy when he tries to prove a drill
instructor who won a Medal of Honor in Vietnam intentionally slew
a Marine recruit.

John Karlen (Sgt. Allistair Adams), Alan Miller (Captain Harry
Collier), James Luisi (Col. Charles Casey), William Smithers (Col.
Hamel).

#56. An Ounce of Prevention
Teleplay by: Steve Greenberg, Aubrey Solomon and Robert Crais
Story by: Steve Greenberg, Aubrey Solomon, Robert Crais, Larry Tuch and Sol Weisel
Directed by: Ken Gilbert

Quincy battles government red tape and a giant corporate power in a desperate effort to save a small town about to be destroyed by a deadly epidemic.

Skip Homeier (Sanders), Dennis Patrick (Larson), Lin McCarthy (Dr. Bellson), Michael Anderson, Jr. (Todd Johnson), Jordan Rhodes (Kent), Booth Coleman (Becker), Mel Carter (EPA Official).

#57. The Death Challenge
Written by: Pat Fielder and Richard Bluel
Directed by: Ron Satlof

An aging magician's comeback is marred when his protégé dies while attempting a water tank illusion trick.

Don Ameche (Harry Whitehead), Ann Blyth (Velma Whitehead), Jo Ann Pflug (Maggie), Ron Masak (Ed Shannon), James Watson, Jr. (Barnes), Bobbi Jordan (Georgette), Martin Kove (Joe Kirby).

#58. The Eye of the Needle
Teleplay by: A. L. Christopher and Robert Crais
Story by: A. L. Christopher
Directed by: Ron Satlof

Quincy must prove that a socialite died as a result of a homicide and not because of a holistic doctor's medical incompetence.

Robert Webber (Dr. Steven Chase), Francis Lee McCain (Dr. Barrie Stoddard), William Sylvester (John Burnett), Anthony James (Hitchhiker), Sally Kemp (Mrs. Burnett).

QUINCY M.E.

Season Four

(1979 –1980)

Episode Titles	Air Dates
59. No Way to Treat a Flower	9/20/1979
60. Dead Last	9/27/1979
61. By the Death of a Child	10/4/1979
62. Never a Child	10/11/1979
63. Hot Ice	10/18/1979
64. Sweet Land of Liberty	10/25/1979
65. Mode of Death	11/1/1979
66. Nowhere to Run	11/8/1979
67. The Money Plague	11/15/1979
68. For the Benefit of My Patients	11/22/1979
69. Murder by S.O.P.	11/29/1979
70. Honor Thy Elders	1/10/1980
71. Diplomatic Immunity	1/17/1980
72. Riot	1/31/1980
73. Cover-Up	2/7/1980
74. Unhappy Hour	2/14/1980
75. The Winning Edge	2/21/1980

#59. No Way to Treat a Flower
Written by: Jeff Freilich and Christopher Trumbo
Directed by: Ray Danton

When Quincy investigates the death of two teenagers who smoked marijuana, he finds it contained a poisonous chemical that is freely available – and that no government agency has stopped its sale or seems to have jurisdiction over it.

Karlene Crockett (Kathy Campbell), Charles Bloom (Joey Campbell), Pat Renella (Ken), Paul Kent (Dr. Osborn), Gary Wood (Ralph Peters), Toni Berrell (Karen Harris), Scott Westlake (Gordon Haight).

#60. Dead Last
Written by: William Zacha and E. Nick Alexander
Directed by: Ray Danton

Quincy investigates a jockey's death which quickly begins to look like homicide.

Joseph Sirola (Ron Henner), Frank McRae (Butterworth), Don "Red" Barry (Charlie), Lou Wagner (Billy McGinn), Howard Dayton (Benny), John Furlong (Dr. Harrison), Ben Marino (Bugs), Austin Willis (Grubb), Daniel Faraldo (Julio Ruis), Richard Balin (Dr. Harper).

#61. By the Death of a Child
Written by: Robert Crais
Directed by: Alan Cook

On a small independent Latin American island, Quincy must determine whether a serum made in America is responsible for the deaths of a number of young children, but his plans and progressive techniques soon stir up religious and political opposition.

Ina Balin (Dr. Maria Pinqera), Robert Loggia (DeVille), David Opatoshu (Boutiere), William Bassett (Harris), Peter Brocco (Advisor), Richard Eastham (Bain), Jay Varela (Dominquez), Arthur Rosenberg (Alan Ross).

#62. Never a Child
Written by: Sam Egan
Directed by: Ray Danton

When a teen falls to her death, Quincy suspects murder as his investigation leads him to a vicious child porno ring.

Cassie Yates (Carol Trager), Alan Manson (Uncle Harry), Melora Hardin (Amanda Colby), Tara Buckman (Terry), Ken Holiday (Father Hamilton), Walter Brooke (Councilman Becker).

#63. Hot Ice
Teleplay by: Robert Crais
Story by: Ralph Wallace Davenport
Directed by: Ran Danton

When Quincy finds diamonds hidden inside a body, he's sent to Las Vegas as an undercover agent and makes everybody nervous with his bungling, including the head of a smuggling ring with whom he makes contact.

John Karlen (Brice), Ed Grover (Niven), Kitty Ruth (Joanie), David Sheiner (Otero), Robert Cornthwaite (Dr. Evans), George Loros (Bernie), Elaine Giftos (Roxie Adams), Nicholas Georgiade (Lew), Charles Picerni (Vito).

#64. Sweet Land of Liberty
Written by: Erich Collier
Directed by: Robert Loggia

Sam Fujiyama becomes deeply disturbed over the strange behavior of an old friend who has turned violent, killed a police officer, and taken his own life. He decides to investigate and help build a case in defense of his friend.

Nobu McCarthy (Lee Yomoshira), Bill Sarto (Steve Yomoshira), Paul Mantee (Perkins), Robert F. Simon (Col. Wilcox), Stack Pierce (Jim Dono), Marcia Rodd (Eleanor Pam-Jansen), Bert Santos (DiGregorio), Logan Ramsey (Capt. Frye), Richard Evans (Col. Flanders).

#65. Mode of Death
Teleplay by: Aubrey Solomon and Steven Greenberg
Story by: Deborah Klugman
Directed by: Rod Holcomb

Quincy orders a psychological autopsy when he can't find conclusive evidence of suicide in the death of a prominent evangelist.

Granville Van Dusen (Kenneth Ross), Marshall Thompson (Dr. Henry), Irene Tedrow (Franklin Osborn), Stephen Elliot (Dr. Chase), Sarah Rush (Lauren), Dan Barton (Mr. Byrne), Regis Cordic (Dr. Condon).

#66. Nowhere to Run
Written by: Sam Egan and Linda Elstad
Directed by: Jeffrey Hayden

When a pregnant teen falls from a cliff to her death, Quincy must determine whether it was murder or suicide as the innocence or guilt of the dead girl's boyfriend hangs in the balance. Then in the course of uncovering the truth, the medical examiner finds some very disturbing facts.

Charles Aidman (Kenneth Watson), Bill Beyers (Jeff Cavanaugh), Mimi Cozzens (Mrs. Cavanaugh), Jack Rader (Mr. Cavanaugh), Dolores Mann (Lorraine Watson), Jennifer McAllister (Cathy Webster), Ben Hammer (Judge Becker), Nancy Carol (Melissa Watson), James Watson, Jr. (Jim Barnes).

#67. The Money Plague
Teleplay by: Sam Egan
Story by: Alan Cole and Chris Bunch
Directed by: Rod Holcomb

When a skyjacker's skeleton is found in a national forest, Quincy's effort to determine the man's identity soon leads to a search for a sinister accomplice and thousands of dollars worth of contaminated money that could cause a deadly international germ epidemic.

Roger Perry (Richard Haber), Henry Beckman (Tom Brady), Robert Hogan (Lt. Dwayne Whitlow), Harry Townes (Dr. McKay), Henry Slate (Sparks), Eric Lawrence (Guardsman).

#68. For the Benefit of My Patients
Teleplay by: Erich Collier
Story by: Erich Collier and Phillip Edelman
Directed by: Jeremiah Morris

When two emergency patients die while being transferred from a private hospital to County Hospital, Quincy takes on the head of the private institution for putting ability to pay ahead of medical concerns.

James Karen (Dr. Rollins), George Deloy (Dr. Varney), Virginia Paris (Dr. Nunez), John Fiedler (County Health Commissioner), Tony Plana (Jorge), Daniel Faraldo (Mando).

#69. Murder by S.O.P.
Written by: Robert Crais
Directed by: Paul Krasny

A fire in the small town jail where Quincy has rested the night claims the lives of four prisoners and the weary medical examiner suspects that it was started to cover up a murder.

John Ireland (Sheriff Evers), Duncan Gamble (Dr. Jessup), Alfred Ryder (Gregory Frost), Edward Andrews (Mayor Joyner), Paul Lambert (Congressman Peters), Ray Duke (Toby), Tom Lowell (Fred), Penny Gillette (Dr. Lathen).

#70. Honor Thy Elders
Written by: Sam Egan
Directed by: Ran Danton

After Quincy traces an old man's suicide to a son's physical abusiveness, he is faced with a similar case involving the exploitation and abuse of two elderly women by their avaricious nephew.

Joby Baker (Timothy Morgan), Susan French (Sylvia Morgan), Julie Adams (Sharon Ross), Barbara Tarbuck (Claire Morgan), Estelle Winwood (Muriel Prentiss), Jessamine Milner (Edna Prentiss), Garnett Smith (Roger Taylor), Anne E. Curry (Mrs. Harper), Leonard Stone (Charles Walter).

#71. Diplomatic Immunity
Written by: Steve Greenberg and Gregory Crossman
Directed by: Ray Danton

When a Latin-American dictator comes to the United States for medical treatment, Quincy must save him from an assassin who has infiltrated the staff of the hospital where he is to undergo surgery.

Rudy Solari (Sarejo), George Wyner (Stewart), Ed Grover (Niven), Valentin de Vargas (Fernandez), Rene Enriquez (Dr. Allermo), Anna Navarro (Isabella Sarejo), Robert Quarry (Ellison).

#72. Riot
Written by: Allan Cole and Chris Bunch
Directed by: Rod Holcomb

When Quincy and Sam go to investigate a prison murder, they are trapped in a riot and held hostage.

John Milford (Warden Tompkins), Taylor Lacher (Bull Stewart), Alan Joseph (Jonah), Al White (Len Woods), Marc Alaimo (Ed Burly).

#73. Cover-Up
Written by: Michael Halperin
Directed by: Paul Stanley

A heart attack victim dies at an emergency hospital because an inexperienced doctor panics and a nurse seeks help from Quincy when she suspects a cover-up.

Margaret Ladd (Nurse Aldred), Dave Shelley (Keane), Michael Durrell (Dr. Edmonds), Nicholas Hormann (Dr. Drew), Lin McCarthy (Dr. Aldred), Norman Burton (Dr. Danner), Colby Chester (Lawyer), Michael Fox (Fire Captain).

#74. Unhappy Hour
Written by: Sam Egan
Directed by: Ray Danton

Teenage alcoholism is involved when a student is killed in a traffic mishap and Quincy must establish whether the niece of his boss Dr. Astin was driving the car and is possibly guilty of manslaughter.

Karlene Crockett (Melody Stedman), Joseph Sirola (Todd Silva), Madlyn Rhue (Laura Stedman), Paul Lambert (Jerry Stedman), Scott Colomby (Eric), Lonny Chapman (White).

#75. The Winning Edge
Written by: Lester William Berke and William Caircross
Directed by: Georg Fenady

When an aspiring Olympic gymnast suffers a fatal fall in practice, Quincy discovers amphetamines in her body and launches an investigation into Coach Virginia Hart's training program.

Caroline Smith (Coach Hart), Jennifer Holmes (Brenda), Doran Clark (Ann Kaiser), Susan Myers (Carolyn), Holly Gagnier (Sherry), Shawn Hoskins (Sally Peters), Lester Fletcher (Pietro), Sandy Balson (Mrs. Peters), Mathew Tobin (Mr. Peters), Shannon Farnon (Mrs. Carmichael).

#76. New Blood
Written by: Jeri Taylor
Directed by: John Peyser

Quincy's vacation replacement – an attractive female doctor –
uncovers evidence of homicide in the "accidental" death of a
prominent politician, and the medical examiner cuts his holiday
short, much to her chagrin, to help in the investigation.

Beverly Sassoon (Dr. Gerrie), Jane Wyatt (Mrs. Bridges), James
Callahan (Councilman Bridges), John Garrett (Davilla), John
Elerick (Fenner), Gloria Manon (Caroline Hughes).

#77. TKO
Teleplay by: Sam Egan
Story by: Sam Egan and Deborah Klugman
Directed by: Lawrence Doheny

When a fighter dies a few days after winning the title, and the chef
at Danny's succumbs to a simple operation, Quincy discovers both
men underwent surgery in the same doctor's private office – an
inadequate facility.

Herbert Jefferson, Jr. (Kenny Mitchell), Sheila DeWendt (Katya),
Kim Hamilton (Mrs. Hester), Frank Maxwell (Dr. Reynolds), Allan
Miller (Dr. Sanders), Robert Hardy (Clarence).

#78. The Final Gift
Teleplay by: Marjorie Worcester and R. A. Cinader
Story by: Marjorie Worcester
Directed by: Georg Fenady

When one of his Korean War buddies dies unexpectedly from injuries sustained in a small plane crash, Quincy traces the cause of death to arsenic poisoning, pointing a finger at the dead man's business partner.

Joseph Campanella (Charlie), Ellen Bry (Linda), Tom Troupe (Max), Don Keefer (Doc Watson).

#79. Deadly Arena
Teleplay by: Sam Egan
Story by: R.A. Cinader and Sam Egan
Directed by: Jeffrey Hayden

When three deaths from botulism are traced to the Coliseum where the world's soccer championship is to take place three days hence, Quincy and an attractive Health Department doctor must find the source of the deadly bacteria before 90,000 spectators are jeopardized.

Diana Muldaur (Dr. Janet Carlisle), Richard Venture (Mr. Mercer), Tammy Lauren (Pele), Mary Carver (Marsha Davenport), Milton Selzer (Ron Jackson), Ray Duke (Arthur Green).

#80. No Way to Treat a Patient
Written by: R.A. Cinader
Directed by: Georg Fenady

A gunshot victim treated by a young doctor at an emergency clinic is dead on arrival at the main hospital from a second wound apparently overlooked at the clinic, and Quincy must find whether the doctor is incompetent or guilty of manslaughter.

A Martinez (Dr. Tony Carbeno), Diane Webster (Nurse Russell), Duncan Gamble (Dr. Sloane), Ana Alicia (Nurse Nancy Berger), Peter Donat (Dr. Warren).

QUINCY M.E.

Season Five
(1980 –1981)

Episode Titles	Air Dates
81. Last Rites	9/16/1980
82. A Matter of Principle	11/12/1980
83. Last Day, First Day	11/19/1980
84. The Night Killer	11/26/1980
85. The Hope of Elkwood	12/3/1980
86. Welcome to Paradise Palms	12/17/1980
87. By Their Faith	1/7/1981
88. Stain of Guilt	1/14/1981
89. Dear Mummy	1/21/1981
90. Headhunter	2/4/1981
91. Scream to the Skies	2/11/1981
92. Jury Duty	2/18/1981
93. Who Speaks for the Children?	2/25/1981
94. Seldom Silent, Never Heard	3/4/1981
95. Of All Sad Words	3/11/1981
96. To Kill in Plain Sight	3/18/1981
97. Sugar and Spice	4/1/1981
98. Vigil of Fear	5/6/1981

#81. Last Rites
Written by: Sam Egan
Directed by Georg Fenady

A small industrial town is opposed to a newly established medical examiner, so Quincy comes to his aid.

William Daniels (Dr. Volmer), Phillip Abbott (William Sullivan), Clifton James (Cliff Webb), Warren Stevens (Wayne Fields), Peg Shirley (Bea Thatcher), Ivan Bonar (Grossland), Bruce Gray (Dr. Miles), Shannon Farnon (Helen Volmer).

#82. A Matter of Principle
Written by: Steve Greenberg and Aubrey Solomon
Directed by: Ron Satlof

Sam Fujiyama develops a process which proves a suspected rapist (named Denbo) can't be guilty because his teeth don't match those which left bite marks on the victims. Then Denbo is arrested a short time later on another rape charge.

Robert Lyons (Bob Denbo), Walter Brooke (Dr. Forbes), Fred Daniel Scott (Judge), John O'Connell (Attorney Arnold), Raymond Mayo (Barton), Wallace Rooney (Dr. Winter).

#83. Last Day, First Day
Written by: Preston Wood
Directed by: Leslie Martinson

Quincy trains a young medical student to be a medical examiner but is shocked and disturbed when she reports that a veteran staff doctor is "covering up" the homicide death of a gangster.

Sarah Rush (Harriet Bolin), Harry Townes (Dr. Moore), Bill Beyers (Tony Moore), Will Kuluva (Rabbi), Maria O'Brien (Ethel Ranier), Seth Wagerman (Joe Ranier).

#84. The Night Killer
Written by: Jeri Taylor
Directed by: Jeffrey Hayden

A young couple discovers one of their twins dead in bed, but through a mishap at the coroner's office, the mother is accused of homicide.

Tyne Daly (Madolyn Estes), Bob Ginty (Bill Estes), Jonathan Segal (Dr. Gage), Patricia Barry (Dr. Hotchkiss).

#85. The Hope of Elkwood
Teleplay by: Michael Braverman
Story by: James Rosin
Directed by: Richard Benedict

The residents of a small college town turn against a track coach accused of negligent homicide, when his alleged brutal training methods are believed to have caused the death of the town's Olympic hopeful.

John Elerick (Benjamin Nicholson), Frank Marth (Coach O'Banion), Charles Aidman (Manning), Clark Mitchell Long (Bobby Nolan), James Rosin (Vic Mascino), Anne E. Curry (Wendy Nicholson), Midge Ware (Jill O'Banion), Fred Pinkard (Theodore Nolan), Pepe Hern (Judge Aquilar), Walker Edmiston (Eliot Martinson), Colin Hamilton (Judge Mallory), Bert Rogal (D. A. Blaine).

#86. Welcome to Paradise Palms
Teleplay by: David Moessinger
Story by: Jon Dalke and Ray Danton
Directed by: Georg Fenady

Quincy rushes to a Native American reservation where his foster son and two others are stricken by bubonic plague. His efforts to control the disease are hampered by greedy resort owners and a Native American medicine man.

Ronald Joseph (Dr. Minnara), Dehl Berti (Shaman), Eddie Garcia (Chester), Joseph Running Fox (Joshua), Dennis Patrick (Charles Curtis).

#87. By Their Faith
Written by: Erich Collier
Directed by: Ron Satlof

Quincy and Sam Fujiyama go to Mexico to assist in determining whether bones found in a car where a young woman is reportedly performing miracles with the sick are actually those of a priest who died in the 17th Century.

Joaquin Martinez (Father Dominguez), Jeffrey Pomerantz (Jensen), Gino Conforti (St. Pierre), Ian Abercrombie (Rutherford), Fay DeWitt (Dr. Berg), Rene Enriquez (Archbishop Vallejo), Eugenia Wright (Jacinta).

#88. Stain of Guilt
Written by: Sam Egan
Directed by: Ray Danton

While working as a technical adviser on a movie based on a famous homicide, Quincy becomes convinced that the socialite convicted of the crime is innocent and he proceeds to prove it with the help of a dedicated lawyer.

Carolyn Jones (Victoria Sawyer), Susan Powell (Cassie Spencer), William Sylvester (D.A.), Ed Begley, Jr. (Kit Sawyer), Martin Rudy (Jason Newland), Bobbi Jordan (Mrs. Newland), Ezra Stone (Judge Simon).

#89. Dear Mummy
Written by: Michael Braverman
Directed by: Georg Fenady

Verification of a mummy involves Quincy with a smuggling ring and a search for Nazi war criminals.

John Karlen (Agent Brice), Ed Grover (Agent Niven), Martine Beswick (Hannah Weiss), Garnett Smith (Mr. Van Dusen), Robert Emhardt (Fresser), Albert Paulsen (Steickler), Than Wyenn (Eichelmann), Ben Frommer (Waiter).

#90. Headhunter
Written by: Fred McKnight
Directed by: Michael Vejar

An airline stewardess romantically involved with a narcotics officer is slain and Quincy's autopsy report brings the police department's internal affairs unit into the investigation.

Joseph Sirola (Lt. Drasso), Eddie Fontaine (Joe Marsala), Suzanne Charney (Nancy Marsala), William O'Connell (Rausch), Lynn Herring (Elaine), Jayne Kell (Leslie).

#91. Scream to the Skies
Written by: Michael Braverman
Directed by: Ron Satlof

Quincy investigates a jetliner crash at sea and discovers that most of the victims died needlessly from hypothermia (rapid lowering of body temperature). This leads the M.E. to fight for better safety precautions all the way to a U.S. Senate committee hearing.

Katherine Justice (Holly), Henry Darrow (Dr. Herrera), Paul Lambert (Senator Hollander), Richard O'Brien (Senator McGreevy), Gilbert Green (FAA Rep. Richmond), Shannon Taylor (Katy Christopher), Stuart Nisbet (Capt. Lawrence), June Dayton (Woman Senator), Charles Lampkin (Dr. Jamison), Nicholas Hormann (Shepherd).

#92. Jury Duty
Written by: Preston Wood
Directed by: Georg Fenady

Quincy serves on a jury in a homicide case and, despite court rules that he is not to use expertise, questions the validity of evidence leading to a mistrial.

Robert Alda (George Temple), Sam Groom (Hillyer), Joan Darling (Judge), Joe Maross (Dr. Morrisey), Morgan Stevens (Frank Munson), Michael Fox (Dr. Feld), John Papais (Len).

#93. Who Speaks for the Children?
Written by: Michael Braverman
Directed by: Georg Fenady

When a 9-year-old girl is slain by a child molester, Quincy uses all his forensic expertise to help a police lieutenant nab the killer who might be the least apparent suspect in the investigation.

Joseph Campanella (Lt. Markosian), Jim Antonio (D. J.), Clyde Kusatsu (Dr. Mitsubi), Allison Balson (Megan), Michele Marsh (Mrs. Carmody), Alex Colon (Carlos), Wendy Lynne (Polly Carmody).

#94. Seldom Silent, Never Heard
Written by: Sam Egan
Directed by: Jeffrey Hayden

A young man is found dead after being chased from a movie theater by angry patrons for bizarre behavior. While police handle the case as a murder investigation, Quincy determines that the victim was suffering from Tourette Syndrome, a rare, often misunderstood neurological disorder characterized by involuntary facial tics, limb movements and verbal outbursts. To make matters worse, it appears the disease is neglected by medical researchers and drug companies who find it unprofitable to manufacture therapies.

Michael Constantine (Dr. Arthur Ciotti), Paul Clemens (Tony Ciotti), Kimberly Webster (Denise), Jon Lormer (William Anders), D. J. Sydney (Mrs. Rosenthal), Dana Gladstone (Mr. Rosenthal), Robert Symonds (Prager), David Tress (Jeffrey).

#95. Of All Sad Words
Written by: Jeri Taylor
Directed by: Bob Bender

Quincy falls hard for a beautiful young widow whose husband died in a night club fire and, despite an autopsy report indicating the death was from natural causes, a persistent insurance investigator accuses her of murder.

Darleen Carr (Elizabeth Chester), Val Avery (Aaron Zacharian), William Wintersole (Morris Gilmour), Borah Silver (Lou Chester), Joseph DiSante (Fire Chief), Peggy Crosby (Waitress).

#96. To Kill in Plain Sight
Teleplay by: Geoffrey Fischer
Story by: Chris Bunch and Alan Cole
Directed by: Ray Austin

Quincy accidentally discovers that the assassination of a government official is planned and he races against time to thwart the plot.

John Ireland (Jerry Driscoll), Fritz Weaver (Sen. Pike), Devon Ericson (Kate Miles), Rafer Johnson (Ezra Glidden), William Prince (Gov. Kain), William Boyett (Sgt. Paul Eckert).

#97. Sugar & Spice
Written by: Jeri Taylor
Directed by: Georg Fenady

Quincy shares the spotlight on a TV talk show with a fad-diet author when, in a burst of anger, he discredits her before a national audience, bringing on a libel suit.

Kathleen Nolan (Corrine O'Connor), Ron Masak (Dick Wilcox), Lisa Jane Persky (Penny Stone), David White (Dr. Fulton), George Petrie (Barnes), Logan Ramsey (Holmes).

#98. Vigil of Fear
Teleplay by: Leo Garen
Story by: Steve Greenberg, Aubrey Solomon and Leo Garen
Directed by: Georg Fenady

Two brothers form a "law and order" vigilante group for their crime-beleaguered neighborhood only to have one of the members kill an innocent man while exchanging gunfire with a robbery suspect.

Lonny Chapman (Officer Spuill), Ned Romero (Ruben Martinez), Henry Slate (Mole), Lenny Bari (Frank Penner), Peter Virgo, Jr. (Tony Penner), Paul Koslo (John Doe killer), George Reynolds (George), Andre Harvey (Jo-Jo).

QUINCY M.E.

Season Six

(1981-1982)

Episode Titles	Air Dates
99. Memories of Allison	10/28/1981
100. The Golden Hour	11/4/1981
101. Slow Boat to Madness (1)	11/11/1981
102. Slow Boat to Madness (2)	11/18/1981
103. D.U.I.	12/2/1981
104. For Want of a Horse	12/9/1981
105. Gentle Into That Good Night	12/16/1981
106. Dead Stop	12/23/1981
107. Bitter Pill	1/6/1982
108. Guns Don't Die	1/13/1982
109. When Luck Ran Out	1/20/1982
110. Smoke Screen	1/27/1982
111. For Love of Joshua	2/3/1982
112. Into the Murdering Mind	2/10/1982
113. To Clean the Air	2/17/1982
114. The Shadow of Death	2/24/1982

#99. Memories of Allison
Written by: Sam Egan
Directed by: Georg Fenady

Quincy falls in love with a beautiful and vulnerable amnesia patient, and the two search her past, uncovering the disturbing fact that a mysterious assassin is out to get her.

Sharon Acker (Allison), Paul Picerni (Sloan), Frank Aletter (Beaudry), Virginia Capers (Sadie), Ivor Francis (Dr. Langley), Art Lewis (Ernie), Martin Rudy (Dr. Selwyn).

#100. The Golden Hour
Written by: Sebastian Milito and Deborah Klugman
Directed by: Georg Fenady

Quincy fights emergency hospital inefficiency after a young girl dies needlessly at a poorly-equipped facility while her father, more seriously injured in the same accident, is saved at a trauma center.

Henry Jones (Supervisor Hawley), Martin E. Brooks (Dr. Fuller), John O'Connell (Dr. North), George Deloy (Mike Harvey), Heidi Bohay (Sherry Anderson), Leonard Stone (Bruce Anderson), Ben Hammer (Marshall), Robert F. Simon (Dr. Fry), Shannon Farnon (Elaine Anderson).

#101. Slow Boat to Madness (Part 1)
Teleplay by: Sam Egan
Story by: Sam Egan and Marc Scott Taylor
Directed by: Daniel Haller

Quincy's ocean-liner vacation turns into a nightmare when sudden mysterious deaths occur aboard the ship and he must find the cause before panic occurs among the 600 passengers.

Diana Muldaur (Dr. Janet Carlisle), Ed Nelson (Capt. Edwards), Linden Chiles (Thomas Ainsley), Mimi Rogers (Corrina), Laurence Haddon (Dr. Linnamen), John Reilly (Flannery), Alan Miller (Dr. Knight), Leslie Winston (Elena), Jack Blessing (Dr. Lindeman), June Sanders (Lorna Ainsley), Flora Plumb (Lyla Crowley).

#102. Slow Boat to Madness (Part 2)
Teleplay by: Sam Egan
Story by: Sam Egan and Marc Scott Taylor
Directed by: Daniel Haller

Quincy and his vacation traveling companion Dr. Janet Carlisle continue to fight a mysterious epidemic that has taken four lives and stricken several more aboard the luxury liner.

Diana Muldaur (Dr. Janet Carlisle), Ed Nelson (Capt. Edwards), Linden Chiles (Thomas Ainsley), Mimi Rogers (Corrina), John Reilly (Flannery), Alan Miller (Dr. Knight), June Sanders (Lorna Ainsley), Jack Blessing (Dr. Lindeman), Adam Klugman (Bartender).

#103. D.U.I.
Written by: Michael Brandman
Directed by: Georg Fenady

When a wealthy attorney uses lax drunk driving laws to avoid punishment after killing a pedestrian, Quincy turns up new evidence at the man's trial which reveals a bizarre scheme aimed at covering up a major crime.

Charles Adman (Preston Claymore), Chevy Colton (Mrs. Levanthal), Randee Heller (Iris), James Watson, Jr. (D. A. Barnes), Ivan Bonar (Dr. Morrow).

#104. For Want of a Horse
Written by: Jeri Taylor
Directed by: Ran Danton

When a kindly landowner is found dead in the wilderness, Quincy's probe uncovers evidence of a homicide and he is challenged to find a suspect and his motives.

Luke Askew (Tanner), Lonny Chapman (Jack), Ronnie Scribner (Gabe), Paul Fix (Randall), Brian Andrews (Andy), Angela May (Georgia), Barbara Tarbuck (Louise Astin).

#105. Gentle Into That Good Night
Written by: Jeri Taylor
Directed by: David Moessinger

Quincy takes over briefly for a thanatologist (one who deals with terminally ill patients) and discovers new meaning in life as the result of his contact with a young mother, dying of cancer, who accepts death.

Tyne Daly (Kay Silver), Spencer Milligan (Steven Silver), Michael Constantine (Dr. Pendleton), Mathew Tobin (Rigoletti), Ken Sansom (Davidson), Stanley Kamel (Dave), Angela Lee (Jenny Silver).

#106. Dead Stop
Written by: Linda Cowgill
Directed by: Ray Danton

Quincy discovers that a trucker's mysterious death was caused by a deadly toxic substance which he had been illegally dumping, and which poses a potential hazard to hundreds of people if they're exposed to it during rainfall.

Salome Jens (Lonny), Jack Ging (Mickey), Gary Wood (Inspector Giavelli), Red West (Harwood), Henry Beckman (Max), Henry Slate (Harold Witten), Tony Burton (Starvin' Marvin).

#107. Bitter Pill
Teleplay by: Sam Egan
Story by: David Chomsky
Directed by: Georg Fenady

After two teenagers die from drug overdoses, both related to the legal but highly dangerous look-alike narcotics, Quincy sets out to shut down the dangerous operation.

Simon Oakland (Zagner), Robert Hooks (Sgt. LeBatt), William Smithers (Sen. Al Stevenson), Ralph Taeger (Coach Chaney), Garnett Smith (Austin Wooster), George Deloy (Mike Garder), Jeb Adams (Craig), Tom Byrd (Perry Jordan), Peggy McCay (Irene Jordan).

#108. Guns Don't Die
Written by: Jeri Taylor
Directed by: Bob Bender

When two unrelated homicides are determined by Quincy to have been committed with the same gun, the medical examiner and police search for the gun which continues to be involved in crimes.

William Sanderson (Willie), Anthony Costello (Slammer), Jody St. Michael (Marco), Lisa Richard (Rae Ann), John Quade (Mel).

#109. When Luck Ran Out
Written by: Paul Haggard Jr. and Jo Lynne Michael
Directed by: Georg Fenady

Nelson Spencer, a friend of Quincy, is suspected of killing his prize race horse and a race track veterinarian to collect two million dollars.

Craig Stevens (Nelson Spencer), Katherine Justice (Annie O'Connor), Chris McCarron (Tommy Canfield), Don Keefer (Dr. Matson), William Wintersole (Winthrop), Ken Scott (Bob Wright).

#110. Smoke Screen
Written by: Michael McGreevey
Directed by: Georg Fenady

Quincy is drawn into a complex arson investigation following a hotel fire in which several people died.

Gerald S. O'Loughlin (Jake Carter), Barbara Stuart (Martha Benedict), Brad Reardon (Andy), Sandy Kenyon (Capt. McKenna), Philip Baker Hall (Capt. Rasmussen), Michael Mullins (Larry

Mitchell).

#111. For Love of Joshua
Written by: Michael Braverman
Directed by: David Moessinger

A drama focusing on Daniel, an 18-year-old with Down Syndrome who proves he can make it in the world, and the progress that's been achieved in the treatment of others afflicted.

Colleen Dewhurst (Dr. Lubow), Tyne Daly (Anna), Clu Gulager (Larry), David MacFarlane (Daniel), Ellen Geer (Dr. Solomon), Ellen Travolta (Mrs. Marguiles), Alan Arbus (Dr. Elerick), Jenny Sherman (Mrs. Darnell).

#112. Into the Murdering Mind
Teleplay by: Michael Braverman
Story by: Linda Cowgill
Directed by: Georg Fenady

Quincy works with the District Attorney in a joint effort to keep a man accused of homicide from being released from custody despite his plea of "not guilty by reason of insanity."

Joseph Sirola (D. A. Angeletti), Henry Darrow (Dr. Hurado), Kelly Ward (Glenn), Conchata Ferrell (Joyce Werner), Lloyd Gough (Judge), Peg Stewart (Nurse).

#113. To Clean the Air
Written by: Sam Egan
Directed by: Les Berke

Quincy battles a small oil refinery violating smog regulations after two people from a sanitarium die from the effects of sulphur pollution.

Stephen Elliott (Graddock), Ronald Joseph (Reuben), Edward Grover (Brisbane), Anthony Eisley (Dr. Ogren), William Sylvester (Torgen), Meg Wyllie (Cleo Erdman).

#114. The Shadow of Death
Written by: Jeri Taylor
Directed by: Georg Fenady

When Quincy investigates the apparent homicide of a nurse who served in Vietnam, he meets the victim's best friend and long-time colleague and discovers that both women have been victims of post-traumatic stress syndrome, and that the surviving woman is in need of treatment.

Karen Austin (Rachel), Sharon Spelman (Chris), Jim Weston (Rod), Paul Jenkins (Kenny), Brendon Boone (Vietnam Veteran).

#115. The Flight of the Nightingale
Written by: Gene Church and E. Paul Edwards
Directed by: William Cairncross

A dedicated nurse is suspended as the result of the death of a patient, prompting a strike at the hospital until Quincy uncovers pertinent evidence.

Georgann Johnson (Nurse Buchanan), James Karen (Dr. Pierce), Patricia Smith (Nurse Mackie), Cynthia Harris (Louise Astin), Peter Hobbs (Bruckner), Will Kuluva (Dr. Howard), Mary Jackson (Mrs. Shanley), Ann Cooper (Nurse Swearingen), Royce Wallace

(Nurse Ruth).

#116. Stolen Tears
Written by: Sam Egan
Directed by: Georg Fenady

A survivor of the Holocaust enlists Quincy's aid in his efforts to track down a Nazi war criminal in the midst of a neo-Nazi movement that denies the Holocaust ever occurred.

Martin Balsam (Chaim), Signe Hasso (Esther), Norman Lloyd (Cornelius Sumner), Michael Durrell (Goldberg), Stefan Gierasch (Wilson), Martin Rudy (Rosenberg), Than Wyenn (Isaac Kroviak).

#117. The Face of Fear
Written by: Michael Braverman
Directed by: Bob Bender

A woman suffering from agoraphobia (fear of leaving one's home) witnesses a murder then tries to overcome her psychological problem to help Quincy and the police nab the killer before she becomes a victim herself.

Carrie Snodgress (Vicki Maguire), Dixie Carter (Dr. Alicia Ranier), Paul Carr (Richard McGuire), Paul Mantee (Ganziano), Jonathan

Frakes (Leon Bohanen), Maria O'Brien (Judy).

#118. Expert in Murder
Teleplay by: Sam Egan
Story by: Marc Scott Taylor
Directed by: Michael Kane

When Quincy testifies that a mobster killed another underworld figure by "scaring him to death," his reputation and testimony are torn to shreds, prompting him to probe deeper into the case to vindicate himself.

Joseph Sirola (Sal Angeletti), Lloyd Gough (Judge Weinecke), Tige Andrews (Victor Ramsey), Robert F. Simon (Sen. Howard Morganthal), Peter Virgo, Jr. (Joseph Ramsey), Irene Tedrow (Mrs. Weinecke).

#119. The Unquiet Grave
Written by: Jeri Taylor
Directed by: Georg Fenady

A former medical doctor and one-time girlfriend of Quincy with a psychotic history is suspected of murdering her wealthy husband.

Ina Balin (Janina Dixon), Cynthia Harris (Louise Astin), John Findlater (Brad Dixon), Georg Gaines (Powell Dixon), Cynthia

Simpson (Carlotta), Vince Howard (Dr. Shiner), David Bond (Mr. Barnes).

#120. The Last of Leadbottom
Written and Directed by: Michael Braverman

While serving as a reactivated Naval Reserve Officer, Quincy is suddenly immersed in a spy mystery involving the sudden death of an admiral at a dedication ceremony.

James Gregory (Admiral Brosnick), Tom Atkins (Commander Butler), Rebecca Holden (Kirsten MacKenzie), Bibi Osterwald (Dorothy MacKenzie), Albert Paulsen (Rear Admiral MacKenzie).

#121. Deadly Protection
Teleplay by: Michael McGreevey
Story by: Michael McGreevey and Fred Long
Directed by: Paul Krasny

When an alleged well-trained guard dog kills the child it was to protect, Quincy investigates and uncovers a vicious racket.

Sam Groom (Jay Stapleton), Jim Antonio (Michael Snyder), Jenny

O'Hara (Evelyn Snyder), Carl Franklin (Redifer), Hoke Howell (Whelan), Nick Georgiade (Bob Gooden), Alex Enberg (Robbie Snyder).

#122. The Mourning After
Written by: Sam Egan
Directed by: Jeri Taylor

Authorities believe a college student committed suicide in the school's swimming pool until Quincy discovers the young man drowned in a lake – the victim of a fraternity hazing.

Carol Rossen (Mrs. Stadler), Robert Hogan (Mr. Stadler), Rosemary Murphy (Dr. Green), Timothy Patrick Murphy (Nick Stadler), Skip Homeier (Dean Ingersoll).

QUINCY M.E.

Season Seven

(1982 –1983)

Episode Titles	Air Dates
123. Baby Rattlesnakes	9/29/1982
124. A Ghost of a Chance	10/6/1982
125. Give Me Your Week	10/27/1982
126. Dying for a Drink	11/3/1982
127. Unreasonable Doubt	11/10/1982
128. Sleeping Dogs	11/17/1982
129. Science for Sale	11/24/1982
130. Next Stop, Nowhere	12/1/1982
131. Across the Line	12/8/1982
132. Sword of Honor, Blade of Death	12/15/1982
133. The Law Is a Fool	1/5/1983
134. Guilty Till Proven Innocent	1/12/1983
135. A Cry for Help	1/19/1983
136. A Loss for Words	1/26/1983
137. Beyond the Open Door	2/2/1983
138. On Dying High	2/9/1983
139. Quincy's Wedding (part 1)	2/16/1983
140. Quincy's Wedding (part 2)	2/23/1983

#123. Baby Rattlesnakes
Written by: Jeri Taylor
Directed by: Georg Fenady

A 14-year-old boy in a program to get kids out of gangs is arrested when a young girl is killed in a drive-by shooting. Quincy believes he's innocent, but if the boy doesn't reveal the shooter, he'll go to prison and jeopardize the program.

Anita Gillette joins the cast as psychiatrist Emily Hanover. Ronald Joseph (Simonetti), Gregory Sierra (Rick Durado), John Randolph (Arthur Degauss), Lynn Hamilton (Mrs. Kellogg), Brendon Boone (D. A.), Arthur Batanides (John Cole).

#124. A Ghost of a Chance
Written by: Steve Greenberg and Aubrey Solomon
Directed by: Ray Danton

Quincy and Sam uncover evidence that a famous surgeon is guilty of "ghost surgery" (allowing another doctor to perform your operation).

Jose Ferrer (Dr. Royce), Nicholas Coster (Ted Markham), Ellen Geer (Mrs. Markham), Phillip Pine (Dr. Panucci), Harry Townes (Dr. Martin).

#125. Give Me Your Week
Written by: Sam Egan
Directed by: Georg Fenady

Quincy and some 500 disabled persons go to Washington to get the attention of an apathetic senator who could hold up important proposed "orphan drug" legislation.

Chris Templeton (Kitty Marinoff), Simon Oakland (Senator Reeves), Joe Campanella (Dr. Styler), Paul Clemens (Tony), Michael Constantine (Dr. Ciotti), Robert Ginty (Brian Marinoff), Peg Stewart (Mrs. Andreas).

#126. Dying for a Drink
Written by: Michael Braverman
Directed by: Georg Fenady

A deputy coroner with a drinking problem that interferes with her work prompts Quincy to suggest she seek help from a recovering alcoholic in the personnel department of the coroner's office.

Ina Balin (Dr. Linderman), David Spielberg (Gary Linderman), Michael Venson (Lawrence), Marge Redmond (Gail Morelli), Maxine Stuart (Margo Hennessy).

#127. Unreasonable Doubt
Written by: Lee Sheldon
Directed by: Richard Benedict

A disabled deputy coroner questions Quincy's belief in the innocence of a father suspected of slaying his brain-damaged child.

John Rubenstein (Dr. Ross), Jim Antonio (Preston), David Sheiner

(Ben Wakefield), David Tress (Judge Parker), Kres Mersky (Lilian Preston), T.J. Castronova (Ed McDonald).

#128. Sleeping Dogs
Written by: Preston Wood
Directed by: Georg Fenady

Several residents of a small community confess to firing the fatal shot at the town bully, and it's up to Quincy to determine how the crime was actually committed.

John Anderson (Police Chief Ollano), Brian James (Henry Moeller), Charles Aidman (Howard Lemner), Sheila Larkin (Jane Lemner), William Bryant (Joe Faraday), George Darcey (J.P. Bumstead), Conlan Carter (Marty Bonham), Jenny Sherman (Judy Fields), Beulah Quo (Mrs. Onoko).

#129. Science for Sale
Teleplay by: Erich Collier
Story by: Diana Marcus, Chris Abbott and Nancy Faulkner
Directed by: Ray Danton

Two bizarre deaths lead Quincy to the discovery of an experiment by a genetic scientist which could be fatal to both the elderly and children if not brought under control.

Lane Smith (Dr. Flynn), Julie Adams (Dr. Winston), Dennis Patrick (Garfield Calhoun), Jason Wingreen (Dr. Freeman), Frank Campanella (Max Wilbur), June Dayton (Judge).

#130. Next Stop, Nowhere
Written by: Sam Egan
Directed by: Ray Danton

Quincy lists punk rock music as a contributing factor in the slaying of a young man — the County Medical Examiner's office is sued for libel and becomes the target of adverse publicity, despite evidence that appears to substantiate the accusations.

Melora Hardin (Abigail), Karlene Crockett (Molly), Kelly Ward (Kip), Barbara Cason (Susan Garvin), Nick Georgiade (Vince Lasker), Amy Moessinger (Pinky).

#131. Across the Line
Written by: Fred McKnight
Directed by: Georg Fenady

A trail of clues suggests that a police officer may have shot an innocent victim at a robbery stakeout to divert his partner's attention during the heist and allow the suspects to escape.

Jack Kehoe (Detective Taggart), Maria O'Brien (Mrs. Taggart), Lonny Chapman (Tourneau), Frank Campanella (Chairman), Spencer Milligan (Capt. Biddles), Ron Pinkard (Det. Jackson).

#132. Sword of Honor, Blade of Death
Written by: Michael Braverman
Directed by: Ray Danton

Quincy and Sam investigate the homicide of a Nisei policeman, a childhood friend of Sam. The trail leads to the Japanese underworld organization, the Yakuza, whose top-level representatives are in America to do business with an organized crime syndicate.

Mako (John Moroshima), Soon-Tek Oh (Capt. Nakatoma), John Fujioka (Nishimura), Richard Lee Sung (Funaki), Donna Benz (Sadako).

#133. The Law is a Fool
Teleplay by: David Karp
Story by: Jack Klugman
Directed by: Georg Fenady

The granddaughter of an esteemed law professor is kidnapped by a former student who wants to trade a one-way trip to Switzerland, complete with bankroll, for the safety of the little girl.

Lew Ayres (Professor Henry Lester Hillman), Jeff Pomerantz (Carl Norman), John O'Connell (Larry Borgassi), Mary Carver (Mrs. Kendall).

#134. Guilty Till Proven Innocent
Written by: Allison Hock
Directed by: Ray Danton

When an innocent family man is subjected to abuse from a grand jury attorney, Quincy tries to defend him with character witness testimony and is sent to jail for contempt.

Rudi Solari (Ted Locke), Eugene Roche (Phillip St. Johns), Susan Plantt Winston (Hannah Locke), Allan Miller (Anawalt).

#135. A Cry for Help
Written by: Jeri Taylor
Directed by: Ray Austin

Quincy gets help from psychiatrist Emily Hanover to learn the truth about whether a teen-age girl's death was suicide or murder.

Thom Bray (Toby Kenyon), Walter Brooke (Judd Kenyon), Sarah Jane Miller (Sarah Kenyon), Megan Wyss (Julie), Dick Gautier (Hale Bonner).

#136. A Loss for Words
Written by: Sam Egan
Directed by: Georg Fenady

Quincy investigates the death in an explosion of a young welder, a high school graduate, whose illiteracy prevented him from reading the danger sign.

Gerald S. O'Loughlin (Chatham), Ramon Bieri (Droyden), Janet MacLachlan (Jill Geary), Rosemary Murphy (Harriett), Charles Knox Robinson (Peter Lassiter).

#137. Beyond the Open Door
Written by: David Moessinger
Directed by: Georg Fenady

A psychic helps Quincy and the police catch a strangler, and the medical examiner is prompted to admit that criminal science may have a new dimension.

Kim Stanley (Edith Jordan), John Furlong (Leon Stimmel), Alex Enberg (Andy Jordan), Christopher Woods (Raymond Pike), Kelly Parsons (Nancy Wallace).

#138. On Dying High
Written by: Michael Braverman
Directed by: Ray Danton

Quincy saves the life of a well-known entertainer who catches on fire while free-basing cocaine, and then learns first-hand about the widespread acceptance surrounding drug abuse.

Roger Miller (J.J. Chandler), Kelly Preston (Ginger Reeves), Edd Byrnes (Bud Auerbach), Henry Beckman (Sgt. Wendorf), James Rosin (Dr. Marty Rothman), Than Wyenn (Dr. Rubinstein), Guerin Barry (Gene), Peggy Crosby (E.R. Nurse), Steven Pringle (Intern), Teresa Hoyos (Nurse).

#139. Quincy's Wedding (Part 1)
Written by: Jeri Taylor
Directed by: David Moessinger

Maximum strains on both Quincy and his bride-to-be, Dr. Emily Hanover, threaten their wedding plans as the big day approaches.

Carole Cook (Winslow), Jeanette Nolan (Edna Brackett), John McIntire (Roy Brackett), Priscilla Pointer (Kathy Benson), Ivor Francis (Dr. Reed).

#140. Quincy's Wedding (Part 2)
Written by: Jeri Taylor
Directed by: David Moessinger

Quincy and Emily patch up their differences and their marriage ceremony goes off on schedule – but just barely – when he is delayed by work in getting to the scene.

June Lockhart (Mrs. Hanover), Carole Cook (Winslow), Jeanette Nolan (Edna), Priscilla Pointer (Kathy Benson), Boyd Bodwell (Richard).

#141. Murder on Ice
Written by: Lee Sheldon
Directed by: Mel Farber

Honeymooners Quincy and Emily find themselves involved in a murder mystery at their Lake Tahoe "hideaway" where their host has also invited other guests, all of whom once participated in a homicide trial.

Lola Albright (Liz McKenna), Dane Clark (Herb Gleason), Ann Blyth (Dorothy Blake), Robert Alda (Lt. Spool), Henry Gibson (Max), Foster Brooks (Petrie).

#142. Women of Valor
Written by: Sebastian Milito and Deborah Klugman
Directed by: Georg Fenady

When a midwife is accused of murder and medical malpractice, Quincy investigates and soon is involved in the hospital-versus-home-birth controversy.

Lynn Hamilton (Olivia), Elizabeth Huddle (Dr. Reid), Philip Abbott (Dr. Wallace), Ivan Bonar (Dr. Block), Frank Birney (Dr. Vale), June Dayton (Mrs. Tracey).

#143. Suffer the Little Children
Teleplay by: David Karp and Neal J. Sperling
Story by: David Karp
Directed by: William Cairncross

When a child dies from abuse and neglect at a camp for orphans, Quincy and Emily set out to close the facility and help a surviving brother of the victim get back home.

Pepper Martin (Ed Rayano), Michele Marsh (Virginia Rayano), Paul Valentine (George Carlton), Tony Dow (Dr. Curtis), Leonard Stone (Mr. Meyers), Paul Lambert (Judge Withers).

#144. An Act of Violence
Written and Directed by: Michael Braverman

Quincy is mugged by two thugs as he follows up on a case, and as a result, suffers extreme emotional trauma.

Brad Gorman (Fox), Alan Stock (Hector), Ed Grover (Schoenbeck), Dana Hansen (Nurse).

#145. Whatever Happened to Morris Perlmutter?
Written and Directed by: Sam Egan

An elderly actor proves that age is not synonymous with senility as Quincy investigates a murder on the basis of an elderly lady's eyewitness identification of a suspect.

Keenan Wynn (Morris Perlmutter), Rosemary DeCamp (Eugenia), Steven Keats (Roland Davies), Louise Fitch (Violet), Woodrow Parfrey (Jimmy). David Sheiner (T.V. Producer), William Sylvester (David Stillwell).

#146. The Cutting Edge
Written by: Jeri Taylor

Directed by: Georg Fenady

Quincy and Emily become involved with a highly advanced medical project when a young worker's severed arm is reattached.

Barry Newman (Dr. Gabriel McCracken), Paul Rudd (Kenny Kelso), John Randolph (Peter Muscanni), Mary Louise Weller (Dr. Wendy Peterson), Allan Fawcett (Dr. Wickett), Ronald Joseph (Paramedic), Chevi Colton (Nurse).

PHOTO SECTION TWO

In his portrayal of Quincy, Jack Klugman's wrath and humanity as an actor were revealed frequently. However, his character's first name was not. The closest viewers came to finding out was a close-up of his business card which showed "Dr. R. Quincy" in "Accomplice to Murder," shown February 3, 1978.

Val Bisoglio in recent years. Often Bisoglio skillfully improvised many of his scenes with series star Klugman and provided a nice diversion from the forensics.

Anita Gillette, who portrayed the spirited Dr. Emily Hanover,
continues to work on stage, in films, and on television.

Ron Satlof, an Academy Award and Emmy Award nominee,
recently directed the film *Misconceptions* on location
in St Petersburg, Florida.

In recent years, Jeffrey Hayden has written, produced and
directed two award-winning documentaries for PBS. He
has also continued to collaborate on theatrical productions
with his wife, actress Eva Marie Saint.

Jeff Freilich (who co-wrote "No Way to Treat a Flower" with Chris Trumbo) with Jack Klugman in 1979.

Jeff Freilich today is executive producer of *Burn Notice* shown on the USA Network.

Emmy nominee Sam Egan was showrunner/executive producer on Showtime/MGM's *The Outer Limits*. Currently, he is the executive producer on *Sanctuary* for the Sci-Fi Channel, and recently he developed *The Listener* for NBC.

After *Quincy*, David Moessinger (shown in early '70s) enjoyed a
lengthy run as an executive producer on popular and acclaimed
series such as *Walker, Texas Ranger, Murder She Wrote, In the Heat of
the Night, Jake and the Fatman,* and *Simon and Simon.*

Following *Quincy*, Michael Braverman was the creator and executive producer of the Emmy Award-winning ABC series *Life Goes On*. As a noted showrunner/executive producer, he has guided such prime time series as *Chicago Hope* and *Beverly Hills 90210*.

Jeri Taylor as creator/executive producer
of *Star Trek: Voyager* in the 1990s.

Marc Scott Taylor (as head of Technical Associates)
continues to consult on occasion for television, movies,
and books dealing with forensic science.

AUTHOR'S TOP THIRTY EPISODES
(in order of broadcast)

Episode	Title	Air Date
7.	The Thigh Bone's Connected to the Knee Bone	2/11/1977
11.	A Good Smack in the Mouth	4/15/1977
16.	Let Me Light the Way	5/27/1977
36.	Requiem for the Living	3/10/1978
37.	The Last Six Hours	9/21/1978
39.	A Test for Living	10/19/1978
41.	Images	11/2/1978
49.	The Depth of Beauty	1/25/1979
50.	Walk Softly Through the Night	2/1/1979
59.	No Way to Treat a Flower	9/20/1979
66.	Nowhere to Run	11/8/1979
70.	Honor Thy Elders	1/10/1980
79.	Deadly Arena	3/27/1980
82.	A Matter of Principle	11/12/1980
84.	The Night Killer	11/26/1980
91.	Scream to the Skies	2/11/1981
93.	Who Speaks for the Children	2/25/1981
94.	Seldom Silent, Never Heard	3/4/1981
99.	Memories of Allison	10/28/1981
105.	Gentle into That Good Night	12/16/1981

QUINCY M.E.

Production Staff
(Partial List)

Creators:	Lou Shaw and Glen Larson
Executive Producers:	David Moessinger 1980-1983
	Robert Cinader 1980
	Donald Bellisario 1979
	Peter J. Thompson 1978-1979
	Richard Irving 1977-1978
	Jud Kinberg 1977
	Glen Larson 1976-1977
Producers:	Sam Egan 1979-1983
	Michael Braverman 1981-1983
	Jeri Taylor 1981-1983
	Lester William Berke 1979-1983
	William Cairncross 1980-1983
	Edward Montagne 1977-1978
	Christopher Morgan 1977
	B. F. Sandefur 1977
	Robert O'Neill 1977
	Michael Sloan 1977
	Lou Shaw 1976-1977

Co-Producer:	Marc Scott Taylor 1982-1983
Associate Producers:	John Hart 1981-1983
	Richard Rabjohn 1979-1981
	Maurice Klugman 1979-1981
	Charles Dismukes 1978-1980
	William Cairncross 1978-1980
	George Crosby 1977-1978
	Gary Winter 1977
	Winrich Kolbe 1976-1977
Cinematography:	Frank Hale 1981-1983
	H. John Penner 1979-1981
	Fred Jackman 1977-1979
	Enzo Martinelli 1977
	Vincent Martinelli 1977
	Ben Coleman 1976-1977
Film Editors:	Jeanene Ambler
	Fred Baratta
	Clay Bartels
	John Dumas
	Richard Freeman
	Buford Hayes
	Douglas Ibold
	Bob Kagey
	Neil McDonald
	Leon Ortiz-Gil
	Richard Rabjohn
	Michael Renaud
	Donald Rounds
	Bernard Small

Assistant Directors:	Bill Carroll
	Phil Cook
	Robert Del Valle
	Carol Lee Emrich
	Dick Erickson
	S. Michael Formica
	Thomas Foulkes
	Doug Gardner
	James Gardner
	Warren Gray
	Gary Grillo
	Ronald Grow
	Richard Hashimoto
	John Liberti
	Ronald Martinez
	Larry Powell
	Mark Sandrich, Jr.
	Albert Shepard
	John Slosser
	Lonnie Steinberg
	Candace Suerstedt
	Robert Villar
	Robert Webb
Second Unit Directors:	William Cairncross
	Roydon Clark
Executive Story Consultants:	Robert Crais
	Jeff Freilich
	David Shaw

Story Editors:	Michael Braverman
	Steven Greenberg
	Michael Kozoll
	Irving Pearlberg
	Aubrey Solomon
	Jeri Taylor
Casting:	William Kenney
	Mary Petterson
	Joe Reich
Technical Advisors:	Dr. Victor Rosen
	Marc Scott Taylor
Art Directors:	Robert Crawley, Sr.
	Bruce Crone
	Ira Diamond
	Alexander Mayer
Set Decoration:	Claire Brown
	Richard DeCinces
	Morris Hoffman
	Joseph Stone
Production Management:	Joe Boston
	Bud Brill
	Phil Cook
	Fred Simpson
	Jack Terry
	Harker Wade
	Rowe Wallerstein
Original Music:	Bob Alcivar
	Bruce Broughton

	William Broughton
	Dick DeBenedictis
	Marvin Laird
	Richard Markowitz
	Vic Mizzy
	Stu Phillips

Music Composers: Glen Larson
                          Stu Phillips

Music Editors: Gene Gillette
                          Arnold Schwarzwald
                          Gerald Tueber

Sound: Albert Cuesta
                          John R. McDonald
                          James Rogers
                          Peter San Filipo, Sr.
                          Edwin Somers, Jr.
                          Jean Valentino
                          Norman Webster

Sound Effects Editors: Jeff Bushelman
                          Barney Cabral
                          Brian Courcier
                          Seth Larsen
                          Joseph Sikorski
                          Clive Smith
                          Don Weisman

Stunt Coordinators: Roydon Clark
                          George Sawaya

Stunts: Gary Downey

Dick Durock
Harold Frizzell
Hubie Kern, Jr.
Gene LeBell
Dennis Madalone
Conrad Palmisano
Charles Picerni

Editorial:	Virgil E. Hammond, III
Transportation:	Chris Haynes
	Dennis Janovic
Camera & Electric Dept.:	Doug Mathias (Gaffer)
	Earl Williman (Gaffer)
	Joe Kelly (Grip)
	Joe August (Camera Operator)
	Howard Block (Camera Operator)
	Frank Hale (Camera Operator)
	Sherman Kunkel (Camera Operator)
Costume and Wardrobe:	Frank Cardinale
	George Whittaker
	Yvonne Wood
Hair Stylist:	Marina Hart

Biographies

Jeanene Ambler

Jeanene Ambler began her show business career as a dancer performing in Las Vegas, on television specials, and on tour with Pearl Bailey. She later became an assistant film editor on such TV series as *Happy Days, Mannix* and *Rockford Files*. Ambler then became a film editor on *Quincy M.E.,* followed by such shows as *Cagney and Lacey, Christie* and *Life Goes On.*

Val Bisoglio

Val Bisoglio, who played the owner of Danny's Place on *Quincy,* once owned a luncheonette in his native New York City.

Bisoglio began his career in the mid-1960s after training in New York at the New School and later at the Actors Studio. In the 1970s and 1980s, he worked with the Colonnade Theatre Lab on New York's upper West Side, which gave unknown actors and playwrights an opportunity.

His feature film work includes *Diamonds, The Frisco Kid, Saturday Night Fever, St. Ives, The Hindenburg, The Don is Dead, The Brotherhood,* and *No Way to Treat a Lady.*

His television credits include *The Sopranos, Life Goes On, Miami Vice, Hill Street Blues, Cover Up, The Fall Guy, M*A*S*H, Galactica 1980, B.J. and the Bear, 240 Robert, Working Stiffs, Flying High, Starsky and Hutch, The Rockford Files, Switch, McCloud, Barney Miller, McMillan and Wife, Matt Helm, Get Christie Love, Police Woman, Baretta, Ironside, Kolchak: The Night Stalker, Kojak, Toma, Columbo, The Bold Ones, The Sixth Sense, All in the Family, The Partridge Family, Longstreet, Mannix, Mary Tyler Moore Show, Bonanza, Hawk, The Nurses* and *Edge of Night*.

Michael Braverman

Two-time Emmy Award nominee Michael Braverman is a 30-year television veteran with hundreds of hours of produced prime time dramas and comedies to his credit. Among his achievements, he was the creator and executive producer of the Emmy-winning ABC television series *Life Goes On*. As a noted showrunner/executive producer, writer and director he has been instrumental in guiding such prime time television series as *Chicago Hope* with David E. Kelley, *Beverly Hills 90120* with Aaron Spelling, *Quincy* with Jack Klugman, and *Higher Ground* starring Hayden Christiansen, Jewel Staite and A.J. Cook. He also wrote and produced numerous television movies including *M.A.D.D. – Mothers Against Drunk Drivers*.

Michael was nominated twice for the prestigious Writers Guild of America Writer's Award as well as the Humanitas Prize, The People's Choice Award and over thirty-five other distinguished professional awards and commendations. Early in his career, he had the privilege of working with such luminaries as Orson Welles and Ray Milland.

Michael is a proud member of the Writers Guild of America, the Directors Guild of America, the Writers Guild of Canada, and ASCAP. He has taught television writing and directing at the extensions of Columbia College of Chicago, UCLA, and UC-Santa Cruz and currently teaches screenwriting, directing, and producing at Academy of Arts University, San Francisco. In his spare time, Michael is completing his second novel.

William Cairncross

William Cairncross began his career as a film editor and subsequent post-production supervisor at Paramount Studios on such series as *Happy Days, The Brady Bunch, Mission Impossible, Mannix* and *Get Smart.*

He later worked as an associate producer, producer and supervising producer on *Life Goes On, Hawaiian Heat, Quincy M.E., Logan's Run, Barbary Coast, The Last Day,* and *The Legend of Lizzie Borden.*

Phil Cook

Phil Cook has worked as an assistant director and production manager in network television for over thirty years. His series and TV movie credits (as an assistant director) include *Diagnosis Murder, A Perry Mason Mystery, Brotherhood of the Gun, Northern Exposure, Desperado, High Desert Kill, Paramedics, Quincy M.E., Shogun, Battlestar Galactica, Kojak, Columbo, The F.B.I., The Fugitive, I Spy, Death Valley Days,* and *Gomer Pyle, U.S.M.C.* As a production manager: *Coach, Aloha Summer, Cover Up, Whiz Kids,* and *Quincy M.E.*

Robert Crais

Prior to his success as one of the industry's top mystery novelists, Robert Crais was an Emmy Award-winning television writer. His credits include *JAG, Earth 2, L.A. Law, Miami Vice, Twilight Zone, The Equalizer, Cagney and Lacey, Cassie & Company, Hill Street Blues, Riker, Quincy M.E.,* and *Baretta.*

Bob Del Valle

Born and raised in San Francisco, Bob Del Valle relocated to Los Angeles where he attended UCLA film school, graduating in 1973.

After gaining experience on a number of low-budget independent projects (amazing the jobs you can get when you're willing to work for free), he joined the Directors Guild of America in 1979. Since then, he has worked as an assistant director, moving up to production manager, and is now also producing.

He was a producer on the HBO television series *Six Feet Under*, on which he worked through its entire run. Additionally, Bob has been involved with various episodic television productions and pilots, including such series as *Swingtown, Shark, The Sopranos, Ally McBeal, Melrose Place, Hunter, Northern Exposure*, and *The Wonder Years*. He has also worked on the PBS miniseries *Tales of the City*, the HBO miniseries John Adams and the ABC 6-hour miniseries Stephen King's *The Shining*. Additionally, he has worked on features, movies-of-the-week, sitcoms, a feature documentary, music videos and commercials.

Bob has been nominated for two Emmy Awards, two Producers Guild of America Awards and is a seven-time nominee for the Directors Guild of America Award, having received one for the pilot of Six Feet Under. His book *The One-Hour Drama Series: Producing Episodic Television* was published in 2008 by Silman/James Press. Bob has been a guest speaker at numerous university television production classes and has also consulted internationally. In addition to the DGA, he is a member of the Producers Guild of America and the Academy of Television Arts and Sciences.

Ira Diamond

Ira Diamond enjoyed a 39-year career as a set designer, art director, and production designer. Some of his many shows include *Fame,*

Dr. Quinn-Medicine Woman, Legacy, Alien Nation, The Rousters, The Islander, Quincy M.E., Kojak, Switch, You Lie So Deep My Love (MoW), The Family Nobody Wanted (MOW), Emergency, Owen Marshall: Counselor at Law, Marcus Welby, Ironside, The F.B.I., McHale's Navy, and feature films such as *Topaz, A Big Hand for the Little Lady, The Andromeda Strain, Airport,* and *Fantastic Voyage.*

Sam Egan

Emmy-nominated writer/producer Sam Egan is currently an executive producer on *Sanctuary* for the Sci Fi Channel and Canada's The Movie Network. He also developed *The Listener* for NBC which premiered in 2009. He was co-executive producer, head writer and showrunner on *Masters of Science Fiction* for ABC – an anthology series featuring Judy Davis, Sam Waterston, John Hurt, Brian Dennehy, Anne Heche, Malcolm McDowell, James Cromwell and Terry O'Quinn, among others.

Egan is best known for his five seasons of work on Showtime/MGM's *The Outer Limits.* He was showrunner/executive producer on the series which ran on Showtime and the Sci Fi channel.

Egan has been a creative consultant on the Canadian series *ReGenesis,* and executive producer on Showtime and MGM's *Jeremiah,* starring Luke Perry and Malcolm-Jamal Warner. An episode he wrote, "Out of the Ashes," garnered Egan the Literacy in the Media Award for Outstanding Television Series in their 4th Annual Awards. Another episode of *Jeremiah,* "City of Roses," was nominated for Canada's Top Ten Writing Awards, honoring the best writing in film and television – Egan's second nomination.

Egan has written *The Volunteer,* a science fiction thriller with Nicholas Cage attached to star for New Line Films. Cage has called Egan "one of the most creative writers of our time. His work on *The Outer Limits* was thought-provoking and inspired." Egan has also written *Across the Universe* for Bill Mechanic's Pandemonium Productions and *Next of Kin* based on the non-fiction work by scientist/pioneer Roger Fouts. Among his notable work was on *The Outer Limits'* 100th episode – "Tribunal" – a time travel story about the Holocaust based on his own father's experiences in Auschwitz, as well as the Showtime movie *Final Appeal,* starring Charlton Heston, Robert Loggia, Amanda Plummer, Hal Holbrook, Cicely Tyson, Swoozie Kurtz, Michael Moriarty, Kelly McGillis, and Wally Langham.

Before his five seasons on *The Outer Limits,* Egan produced and wrote CBS's *Northern Exposure.* Egan also created two series for CBS: *Snoops* starring Tim Reid and Daphne Maxwell Reid, and *Sweating Bullets,* which ran three seasons on the network.

He was the writer/producer of *The Kid Who Loved Christmas* for Eddie Murphy Productions and Paramount (Sammy Davis Jr.'s last film), which co-starred Vanessa Williams, Cicely Tyson, and Esther Rolle.

Egan co-wrote and co-produced *Imagine – John Lennon,* a Warner Bros. documentary feature.

Included in Egan's many writing and producing awards are nominations for an Emmy and four Geminis. He is also the winner of the Edgar Award from the Mystery Writers of America.

Don Eitner

Don Eitner began his theatrical career in the mid-1950s, starring in the pilot film for the television series *West Point.* He went on to appear in more than 80 network television shows including *Dallas, Dynasty, Quincy M.E., Harry O, Owen Marshall: Counselor at Law, Mission Impossible, The F.B.I., The Invaders,* and *The Fugitive.*

In the mid-'60s, he began teaching and directing at the Melrose Theater, where he staged 22 productions. Eitner subsequently founded and became the artistic director of American Theater Arts in Los Angeles which produced more than 50 plays, and trained several hundred aspiring professional actors.

As a guest director at the Dallas Theater Center, Eitner staged the critically acclaimed *Diary of a Madman* and *The Lion in Winter*, and would later return to Texas to become the General Manager and Artistic Director of the Corsicana Community Playhouse.

Upon his return to California, Eitner directed several productions at the Fullerton Civic Light Opera, and became the theatre arts instructor for the Southern California Music Theatre Association's summer program for youth.

In recent years, he has directed a revised version of *Diary of a Madman* and the award-winning one-woman production of Mariette Hartley's *If You Get to Bethlehem, You've Gone Too Far*.

Jeff Freilich

Jeff Freilich is currently the executive producer/director of *Burn Notice*, the Fox television series shown on the USA Cable Network, and has enjoyed a lengthy career in network television.

After attending medical school, Freilich decided to focus on a writing/producing career. At the American Film Institute he produced Tim Hunter's thesis film *Devil's Bargain*, after which he worked for producer Roger Corman and co-wrote (with Hunter) a rewrite of the movie *Hollywood Blvd.* (the first film of Joe Dante and Alan Arkush).

After writing several westerns in Mexico, Freilich began his career in television writing for series such as *Doctor's Hospital, Baretta, Quincy M.E.,* and *Mrs. Columbo.* He subsequently became a writer/producer on *The Incredible Hulk* and *Galactica 1980*.

A partial list of his many television credits as a writer/producer, director, creator and executive producer include *Behind Enemy Lines: Columbia, Code Name: Phoenix, Execution of Justice, Naked City: A*

Killer Christmas, Naked City: Justice With a Bullet, Rescuers: Stories of Courage, Against the Grain, Dark Justice, Freddy's Nightmare, Falcon Crest, Knots Landing, and *Flamingo Road.*

Anita Gillette

Broadway veteran and Tony-nominated actress Anita Gillette has also had a lengthy career in television and feature films. Her motion picture credits include *Shall We Dance, Moonstruck, Boys on the Side, Bob Roberts, Larger Than Life, The Guru, She's the One, The Great New Wonderful,* and the upcoming *Hiding Victoria* and *The Last Adam.*

Her television credits include *30 Rock, Women's Murder Club, CSI, Queens Supreme, The War at Home, Law and Order: Criminal Intent, George M., Sex and the City, Frasier, A Christmas Memory, Law and Order, Mad About You, Almost Grown, Brothers, You Again, Brass, Another World, Marathon, The Baxters, Trapper John M.D., Quincy M.E., It Happened at Lakewood Manor, All That Glitters, A Matter of Wife . . . and Death, Love American Style, Bob & Carol & Ted & Alice, Honeymoon Suite, Me and the Chimp,* and *Normal, Ohio.*

Jeffrey Hayden

Jeffrey Hayden has directed more than 400 television shows for the major networks, including *In the Heat of the Night, Magnum, P.I., Cagney & Lacey, Quincy M.E., Ironside, Mannix, Palmerstown, The Bold Ones, Peyton Place, Route 66, 77 Sunset Strip, The Andy Griffith Show, The Donna Reed Show,* and *Leave it to Beaver,* among others.

After graduating from the University of North Carolina, Chapel Hill, he went to New York, where he directed many live shows in the "Golden Age of Television," including *Omnibus, NBC Color Specials,* and *The Philco-Goodyear Playhouse,* where he directed Paul Newman, Inger Stevens, Walter Matthau, E. G. Marshall, and James Dean, in powerful dramatic roles. This led to an invitation to join MGM in Hollywood where he directed his first feature film, The Vintage.

Along with his film and television work, Mr. Hayden continued producing and directing in the theatre: *Summer & Smoke, Desire Under the Elms, The Fatal Weakness, Candida, Dark a the Top of the Stairs, Awake and Sing, The Country Girl, Duet for One, The Front Page, Death of a Salesman, The Sunshine Boys,* in New York, at the Kennedy Center, Los Angeles, and regional theaters around the country.

More recently he wrote, produced, and directed two award-winning documentaries for *PBS: Primary Colors: The Story of Corita,* and *Children in America's Schools* with Bill Moyers. They earned him an Emmy, Cine Golden Eagle, AFI Award, the Edward R. Murrow Award, and the NEA's Golden Medal. Other awards for his television work include the California Governor's Media Award, the Robert E. Sherwood Award, and the NAACP Image Award.

Married to Eva Marie Saint since 1951, they have collaborated on many theatrical productions and continue to do so in *Love Letters* and *On the Divide: The Works of Willa Cather,* with Mr. Hayden co-starring as well as directing.

Robert Ito

Born in Vancouver, British Columbia, Robert Ito began his career as a dancer with the National Ballet of Canada. Eventually he went to New York and landed a featured role in the Broadway hit *Flower Drum Song,* followed by a part in the original cast of *What Makes Sammy Run.*

Ito moved to Los Angeles in the mid-60s and began to win roles in episodic television shows. His numerous TV credits include *Justice League, Myth Quest, Star Trek: Voyager, The Immortal, The King of Queens, Dr. Quinn: Medicine Woman, Superman, The Hunger, Johnny Quest: The Real Adventures, Chicago Hope, Once a Thief, The Outer Limits, Iron Man, One West Waikiki, The X Files, Kung Fu: The Legend Continues, Vanishing Son, Gargoyles, Highlander, The Commish, Renegade, MacGyver, Falcon Crest, Tour of Duty, Star Trek: The Next Generation, Knots Landing, Airwolf, Magnum P.I., B.J. and the Bear, How the West Was Won,*

M*A*S*H, Barnaby Jones, Helter Skelter, Harry O, Kojak, Kung Fu, Marcus Welby M.D., Love American Style, Mannix, Ironside, It Takes a Thief, Get Smart and *I Spy.*

Feature films include *The Omega Code, Samurai Swing, Hollow Point, The Vineyard, Aloha Summer, Pray for Death, Gray Lady Down, Black Sunday, Midway, Rollerball, The Terminal Man,* and *Soylent Green.*

Jack Klugman

Jack Klugman, a three-time Emmy Award winner, has won acclaim for his work on stage and screen as well as on television.

After studying drama at Carnegie Tech in Pittsburgh, Klugman went to New York where he played roles in many off-Broadway and summer stock productions before making his Broadway debut. His television career began in the golden age of the 1950s live drama. His portrayal of a blacklisted actor in an episode of *The Defenders* brought him his first Emmy in 1963. Two others came in 1971 and 1973 in *The Odd Couple,* the hit comedy series in which he portrayed sports writer Oscar Madison opposite Tony Randall as Felix Unger.

His many television credits include *Presidio Med, Crossing Jordan, Third Watch, The Outer Limits, Diagnosis Murder, The Odd Couple: Together Again, The Love Boat, One of My Wives is Missing* (MOW), *The Underground Man* (MOW), *Banyon, Love American Style, The Name of the Game, The Bold Ones, The F.B.I., Then Came Bronson, Garrison's Gorillas, I Dream of Jeannie, Ben Casey, The Fugitive, Harris Against the World, The Great Adventure, Arrest and Trial, Naked City, The Untouchables, Cain's Hundred, The New Breed, Follow the Sun, General Electric Theater, Gunsmoke,* and *Alfred Hitchcock Presents.*

His feature film work includes *Two-Minute Warning, Goodbye Columbus, The Detective, Act One, I Could Go on Singing, Days of Wine and Roses, Cry Terror, 12 Angry Men* and *Timetable.*

Glen Larson

In the 1970s and 1980s, Glen Larson emerged as one of the most prolific producers in Hollywood. He created, co-created and was the executive producer of many well-known prime time TV series featuring action, adventure, and comedy while providing family entertainment.

Early in his career he worked as a writer, associate producer and producer on *It Takes a Thief* and *Alias Smith and Jones*.

Larson was also musically talented, and was an original member of the Four Preps in the late 1950s. In later years, he would compose the theme music for many of his weekly TV shows.

Some of his best known television series include *Knight Rider, The Fall Guy, One West Waikiki, Battlestar Galactica, Buck Rogers in the 25th Century, B.J. and the Bear, The Misadventures of Sheriff Lobo, The Hardy Boys/Nancy Drew Mysteries, Quincy M.E., McCloud* and *Switch*.

David Moessinger

David Moessinger has had a long and varied career in the television industry, wearing the hats of writer, director, and producer.

He was executive producer on many popular and acclaimed series, including *Walker, Texas Ranger, Murder She Wrote, In the Heat of the Night, Jake and the Fat Man, Simon and Simon, Blue Thunder,* and *Quincy M.E.*

As a writer and director, he worked on such shows as *Eight is Enough, Father Dowling, Knots Landing, Kung Fu, The Wild Wild West, Serpico, Kraft Suspense Theater, Mission Impossible, Police Woman* and *Police Story*. He also wrote the motion picture *Number One,* starring Charlton Heston.

During his years in the industry, Moessinger received two Emmy nominations, a People's Choice nomination, two Gabriel Awards, a

Scott Newman Award, plus citations from the Arthritis Foundation and American Women in Radio and Television.

Moessinger graduated from DePauw University in 1952 with a Bachelor of Arts degree. He was a member of Phi Kappa Psi Fraternity and lettered in football. After graduation he served as an officer in the United States Marine Corps before beginning his career in television.

He is now retired and lives in Northern California with his wife, Jeri Taylor, and two cats.

John S. Ragin

After graduating from Carnegie Tech in Pittsburgh, John Ragin studied in London on a Fulbright scholarship and later with Lee Strasberg and Sandford Meisner in New York.

Ragin's theater background includes Shakespeare and the classics. He performed in *Macbeth* and *The Winter's Tale* with the New York Shakespeare Festival, and did *Antony and Cleopatra, The Tempest* and *All's Well That Ends Well* with the Shakespeare Festival in Stratford, Connecticut.

His motion picture credits include *Earthquake, The Parallax View, Marooned, Doctors' Wives, Bob & Carol & Ted & Alice,* and *I Love You, Alice B. Toklas.*

On television his appearances include *Star Trek: The Next Generation, Santa Barbara, Airwolf, Murder, She Wrote, Riptide, Emerald Point N.A.S., B.J. and the Bear, The Islander, The Amazing Howard Hughes, City of Angels, Jigsaw John, Harry O, McCloud, Barnaby Jones, Switch, Delancey Street, The Rookies, Cannon, Sons and Daughters, Senior Year, The F.B.I., The Magician, Love is Not Forever, Mannix, Cool Million, Ironside, Alias Smith and Jones, The Bold Ones, The Forgotten Man, Storefront Lawyers, Night Gallery, Mission Impossible, The Most Deadly Game, The Lonely Profession, Get Smart,*

The Whole World Is Watching, Felony Squad, The Outsider, Wild Wild West, The Invaders, Love on a Rooftop, Laredo, Gomer Pyle, U.S.M.C., Not For Hire, and *Alfred Hitchcock Presents.*

Joe Reich

Joe Reich was a well-known casting director for over 35 years with over 2500 hours of network credits. A graduate of Carnegie-Mellon University Drama School, his career started in the infamous mail-room – this one at Universal. During his long-term stint at Universal he cast series, MOWs, pilots, etc. He ran the casting gamut – everything from *Jack Benny* and *McHale's Navy* to *Alfred Hitchcock Presents, The Virginian* to *Quincy M.E.,* as well as shows like *The Six Million Dollar Man, Simon & Simon, Knight Rider,* and *Airwolf.*

Leaving Universal to form his own casting company, Joe Reich & Friends, over the next few years he cast several features, including the now famous cult film, *The Beastmaster.* He then returned to Universal for a two-year period as a staff casting director. He then became director of casting for *The Arthur Company,* casting *Airwolf II* in both LA and Canada.

He was appointed head of casting for the NBC daytime drama *Generations* and then became director of casting for Reg Grundy Productions assigned to cast the syndicated prime-time serial *Dangerous Women.* After that he formed Quantum Casting with a partner, and cast various projects, i.e., features, an MOW for NBC, a half-hour comedy pilot, and an interactive CD-ROM for *Interplay.*

One of the three founding members of The Casting Society of America, he is also a long-time lecturer and teacher at local colleges and drama schools and recently taught improvisation and cold-reading classes for a private school at CBS over a three year period. He also conducts audition improv workshops for AFTRA.

He is past-President of Theater East Professional Workshop,

and a past 20-year member of the director's unit. No longer actively casting, his current assignment (for the past 13 years) is senior manager in the Casting Administration Department at Disney, solely responsible for the television animation section of the department.

Joseph Roman

At age 15, Joseph Roman became the youngest instructor in Philadelphia's YMCA program, and at age 17 owned his own gym. In his spare time, he studied at the Dramatic Workshop, and later moved to New York to study with Lee Strasberg.

Roman made his Broadway debut in *Mr. Roberts*, followed by *Twilight Walk* with Walter Matthau, and *Child of the Morning* with Margaret O'Brien.

He arrived in Hollywood in the mid-1970s. His film work includes *Bugsy, Murphy's Law, Love and Bullets, Run for the Roses, The White Buffalo*, and *St. Ives*.

Television appearances include *You Again?* (recurring), *Quincy M.E.* (as Sgt. Brill), *Columbo: Last Salute to the Commodore, Decoy, You Are There*, and *Studio One*.

Ron Satlof

Born and raised in New York City, Ron Satlof is an Academy Award and Emmy-nominated director and producer who has worked in film and television as well as repertory theatre. A graduate of Carnegie-Mellon University, he began his film career as a trainee assistant director.

Long active in network TV as a producer and director, Ron produced the long-running, top-ten TV series *McCloud* with Dennis Weaver, for which he received an Emmy nomination, and directed episodes of such classic shows as *Hawaii Five-O, Quincy M.E.* and *Barnaby Jones*.

Ron was a contract director at Columbia Pictures Television

where, among other projects, he directed a two-hour TV production of *From Here to Eternity* with Don Johnson, Kim Basinger, Barbara Hershey and William Devane. Ron's picture *Spiderman Strikes Back*, which he produced and directed, was distributed in Europe, Asia and South America by Columbia Pictures International. He has directed such TV productions as *Perry Mason Returns*, *Diagnosis Murder*, *Martial Law*, and *Silk Stalkings*. TV pilots he directed include *Jake and the Fatman* with William Conrad, and *Hunter* with Fred Dryer. He also directed the TV movie *Original Sin* with Charlton Heston and Ann Jillian.

He received an Academy Award nomination for his live action short *Frog Story*, which he co-produced and directed.

Lou Shaw

Lou Shaw has written and produced a variety of network television series in addition to having enjoyed success as an award-winning playwright, novelist, and theatrical producer.

His 200 television credits include *The Fall Guy* (also produced), *Cover Up*, *The Hardy Boys/Nancy Drew Mysteries* (also produced), *Quincy M.E.* (co-creator/producer), *The Misadventures of Sheriff Lobo*, *Beyond West World* (also creator/executive producer), *The Six Million Dollar Man*, *Columbo*, *Switch*, *McCloud* (also produced), *Ironside*, *Chase*, *Mannix*, *Love American Style*, *Mission Impossible*, *Search*, *Maude*, *Barnaby Jones*, *The Bill Cosby Show*, *The Virginian*, *Hawk*, *12 O'Clock High*, *The Donna Reed Show*, *Branded*, *The Munsters*, *Ben Casey*, *Naked City*, *The Rebel*, *Alfred Hitchcock Presents*, *Rawhide*, *Wagon Train* and *The Millionaire*.

Jeri Taylor

Jeri Taylor graduated from Indiana University with an AB degree in English with a heavy focus on theater and television. In Los Angeles she worked extensively in equity waiver theater as an actress, director and teacher of acting. All of her background coalesced when she embarked on a career as a writer/producer/director in television.

Her credits include such shows as *Little House on the Prairie, The Incredible Hulk, Quincy M.E., Magnum P.I., In the Heat of the Night, Jake and the Fatman,* and *Murder, She Wrote.* She ended her career with a tenure of eight years on the Star Trek franchise, writing and serving as executive producer for *Star Trek: The Next Generation* and *Star Trek: Voyager,* which she co-created.

Marc Scott Taylor

Marc Scott Taylor is President and laboratory director of Technical Associates, Inc. located in Ventura, California. A forensic scientist for 35 years, he has specialized in forensic DNA analysis for the past 18 years. A member of the American Academy of Forensic Sciences (AAFS) and the California Association of Criminalistics (CAC), Marc is certified as DNA Technical Leader/Technical Manager by the American Society of Crime Laboratory Directors (ASCLD).

Technical Associates was one of the first laboratories to use polymerase chain reaction (PCR)-based DNA analysis in forensic casework. Marc has been a consultant on many high-profile cases involving DNA analysis performed at Technical Associates as well as other laboratories. He has been court-qualified as an expert in DNA analysis, GSR analysis, and general criminalistics in over 40 states as well as overseas, in both civil and criminal cases. The staff at Technical Associates, Inc. is routinely involved in education through lectures to college classes and an active internship program. Technical Associates, Inc. educates attorneys in the meaning and use of DNA evidence in criminal and civil cases.

Marc continues to consult on occasion for television, movies and books dealing with forensic science. With the staff at Technical

Associates, Inc. he has participated in news presentations for network news programs and the Discovery Channel.

Christopher Trumbo

Chris Trumbo has worked as a writer for the motion picture, television, theatre, and print media for more than 40 years. He is particularly proud of the television movie *Ishi, The Last of His Tribe* on which he shares a credit with his father, Dalton Trumbo.

Harker Wade

Harker Wade began his career as an assistant director on television series such as *Combat, The Virginian* and *Adam 12*. His credits as a producer, co-producer and supervising producer include *Sleepwalkers, The Visitor, The Burning Zone, Sea Quest DSV, L.A. Fire Fighters, Crowfoot, Quantum Leap, A Burning Passion: The Margaret Mitchell Story, Tequila and Bonetti, In Like Flynn, Knight Rider, Rooster, The Fall Guy, Buck Rogers in the 25th Century, Battlestar Galactica, Quincy M.E., McCloud,* and *Owen Marshall: Counselor-at-Law.*

Garry Walberg

Garry Walberg enrolled at the Studio Theater School in his native Buffalo, New York while still in his teens. After two years of study, he went to New York City. Eventually Walberg enrolled at the American Theater Wing. From there he began to work in summer stock and landed parts in live television shows.

Walberg arrived in Hollywood in the late 1950s. His many television appearances include: *The Odd Couple: Together Again, Murder, She Wrote, Hardcastle and McCormick, The Amazing Howard Hughes, Amelia Earhart, Cannon, Starsky and Hutch, Lucas Tanner, The Rockford Files, Mannix, The Waltons, Gunsmoke, Police Woman, Kojak, Love American Style, The Odd Couple, Banacek, Columbo, The*

High Chaparral, The Mod Squad, Then Came Bronson, Bonanza, Green Acres, Land of the Giants, The Fugitive, Run for Your Life, Star Trek, The F.B.I., The Virginian, Peyton Place, Lassie, Ben Casey, Dr. Kildare, Perry Mason, Combat, Rawhide, Outlaws, M Squad, and The Twilight Zone.

His film credits include MacArthur, Two-Minute Warning, King Kong, When the Legends Die, The Man, The Organization, The Andromeda Strain, They Call Me Mr. Tibbs, Tell Them Willie Boy Is Here, The Maltese Bippy and Charro.

ENDNOTES

Telephone Interviews by the Author and Other Sources

1. Lou Shaw, December 2008, California

2. Jack Klugman ("What Kind of Doctor Goes Around Hitting People?" Bill Davidson. TV Guide, March 12, 1977).

3. Jack Klugman ("Klugman as Quincy: Make it Relevant," Cecil Smith. Los Angeles Times, February 20, 1977).

4. John S. Ragin, December 2008, California

5. Robert Ito ("Rubbing Quincy the Right Way," Bill O'Hallaren. TV Guide, January 19, 1980).

6. Val Bisoglio, December 2008, California

7. Joe Reich, December 2008, California

8. Anita Gillette, January 2009, New York

9. Phil Cook, December 2008, California

10. Ron Satlof, December 2008, Florida

11. Bob Del Valle, December 2008, California

12. Ira Diamond, December 2008, California

13. Marc Scott Taylor, December 2008, California

14. Marc Scott Taylor ("Quincy's Biggest Lab Experiment," Rona Lee Kleiman, TV Guide, December 5, 1981).

15. Harker Wade, January 2009, California

16. William Cairncross, December 2008, California

17. Jeffrey Hayden, December 2008, California

18. Jeff Freilich, December 2008, California

19. Christopher Trumbo, December 2008, California

20. Jack Klugman ("Conversation with Klugman," John Connell. Reel, Vol. II, Winter 1978).

21. Sam Egan, January 2009, California.

22. David Moessinger, January 2009, California

23. Michael Braverman, January 2009, California

24. Jack Klugman ("Quality TV: Just a Matter of Time," Susan Christian, Los Angeles Herald Examiner, February 9, 1981).

25. Jack Klugman ("Quincy: Mirror of an Assassin," Lee Margulies, Los Angeles Times, July 7, 1982).

26. Jeri Taylor, January 2009, California

27. Don Eitner, January 2009, California

28. Jeanene Ambler, January 2009, California

About the Author

Born and raised in Philadelphia, James Rosin graduated from Temple University's School of Communications with a degree in broadcasting. In New York he studied acting with Bobby Lewis and appeared in plays off-off Broadway, in New England summer stock, and on the ABC soap opera *Edge of Night*. In Los Angeles Rosin played featured and co-starring roles on TV in *Mickey Spillane's Mike Hammer, T.J. Hooker, Quincy M.E., The Powers of Matthew Star, Cannon, Mannix, Banacek, Adam-12, Love American Style*, and two miniseries, *Loose Change* and *Once an Eagle*.

His film credits include *One Fine Day, Up Close and Personal, Sleepers, Night Falls on Manhattan*, and *The Adventures of Buckaroo Banzai*. He also wrote stories and teleplays for *Quincy M.E.* (NBC), *Capitol* (CBS) and *Loving Friends and Perfect Couples* (Showtime). His full-length play, *Michael* in *Beverly Hills*, a comedy-drama, premiered at American Theater Arts in Los Angeles and was later presented off-off Broadway at the American Musical Dramatic Academy's Studio One Theater.

In recent years, Rosin has written and produced two one-hour sports documentaries which have aired on public television: *Philly Hoops: The SPHAS and Warriors* (about the first two professional basketball teams in the City of Philadelphia) and *The Philadelphia Athletics 1901-1954* (about the former American League franchise). His first book, *Philly Hoops: The SPHAS and Warriors* was published in 2003, followed by *Rock, Rhythm and Blues* (2004), Philadelphia: *City of Music* (2006), *Route 66: The Television Series 1960-1964* (2007), *Naked City: The Television Series* (2008), *Wagon Train: The Television Series* (2008), and *Adventures in Paradise: The Television Series* (2009).

He has also been a contributing writer to *Classic Images* and *Films of the Golden Age* magazine.

CPSIA information can be obtained
at www.ICGtesting.com
Printed in the USA
BVOW10s0755190217
476261BV00009B/222/P